AF480207

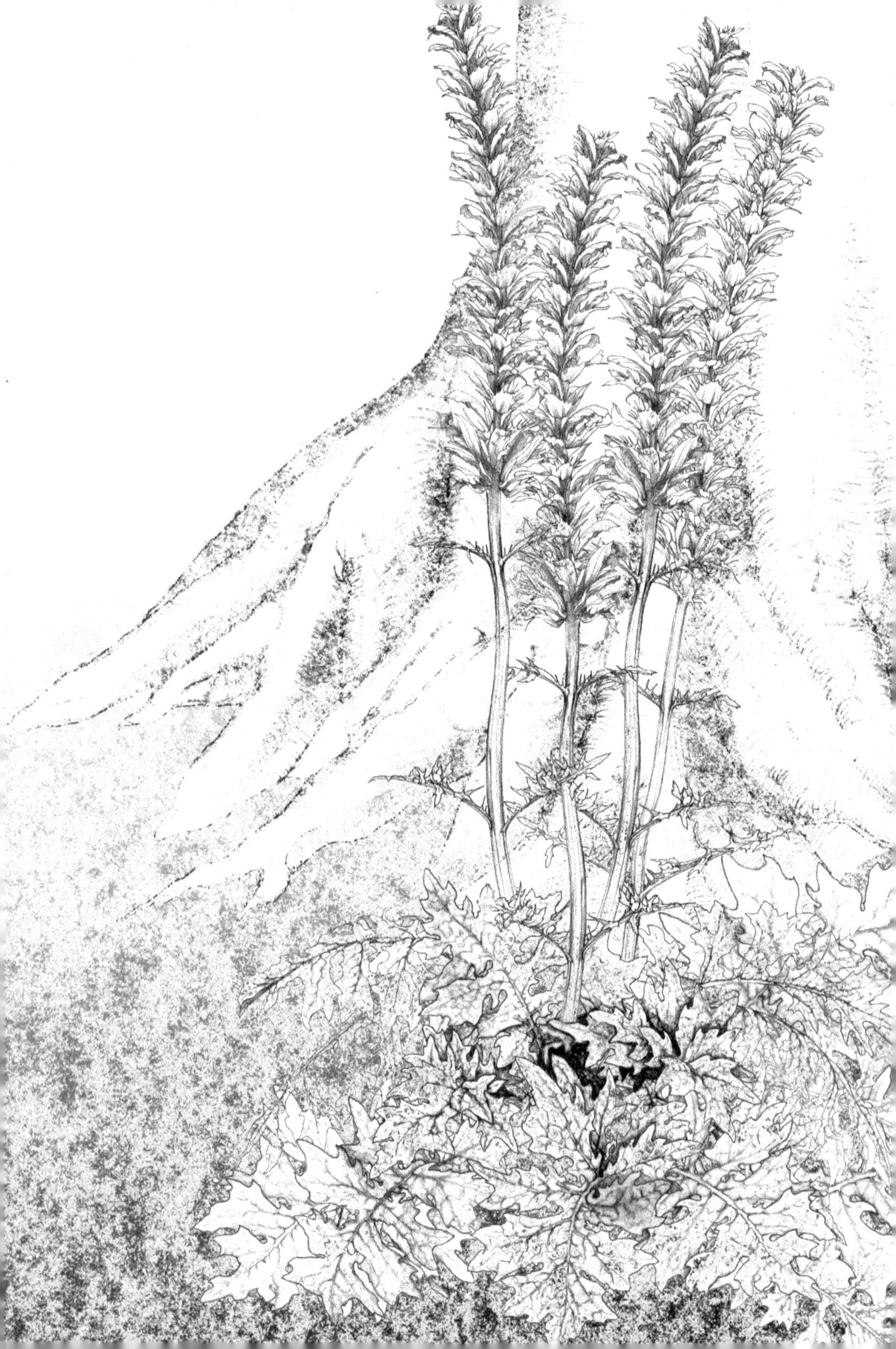

the way things are

WALLY GILBERT

The room was vacant,
though no sign displayed,
when she pushed at the open door.
Since then the vacancy is filled,
though no one lives there still.
Outside the windows people pass,
laughing in the sunshine.

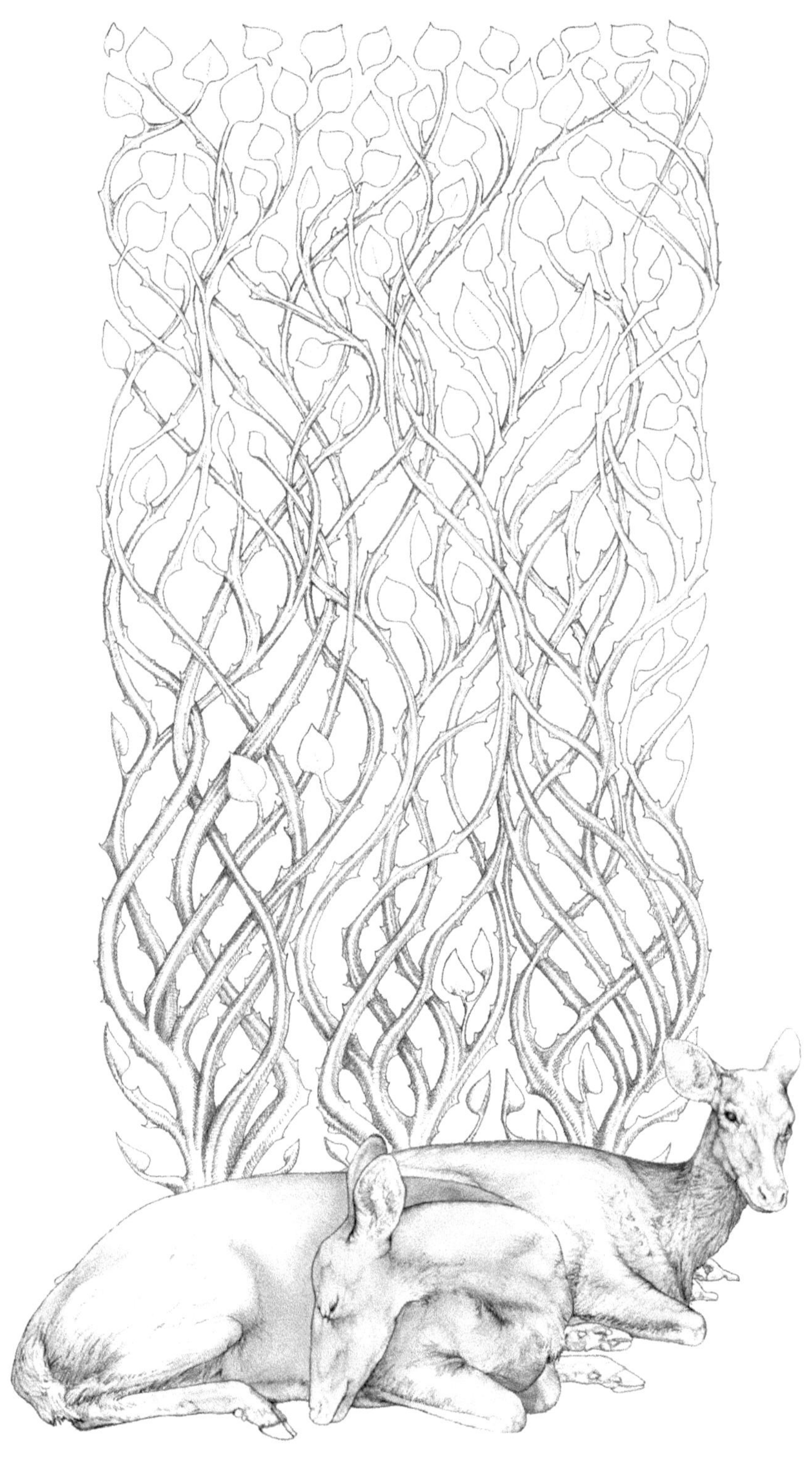

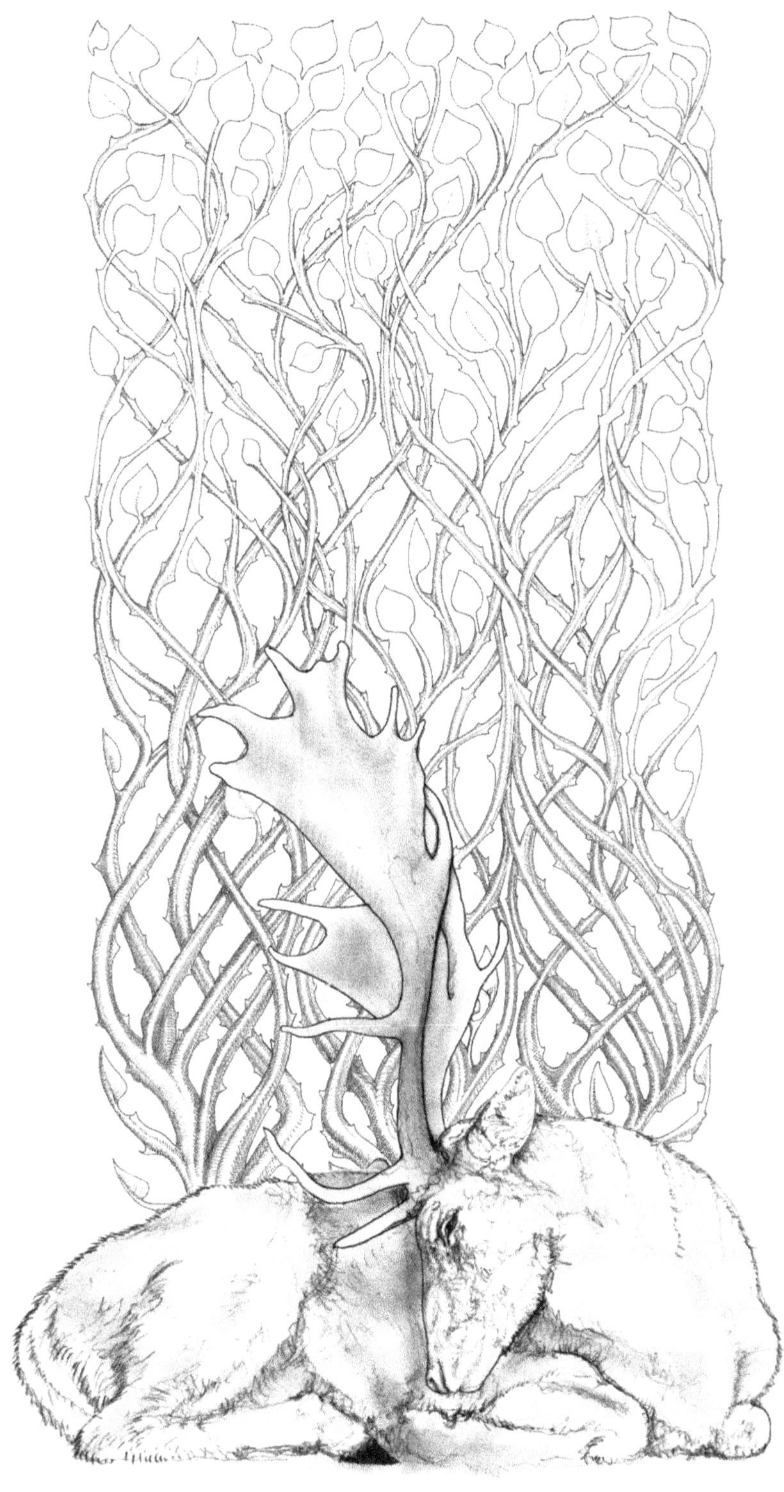

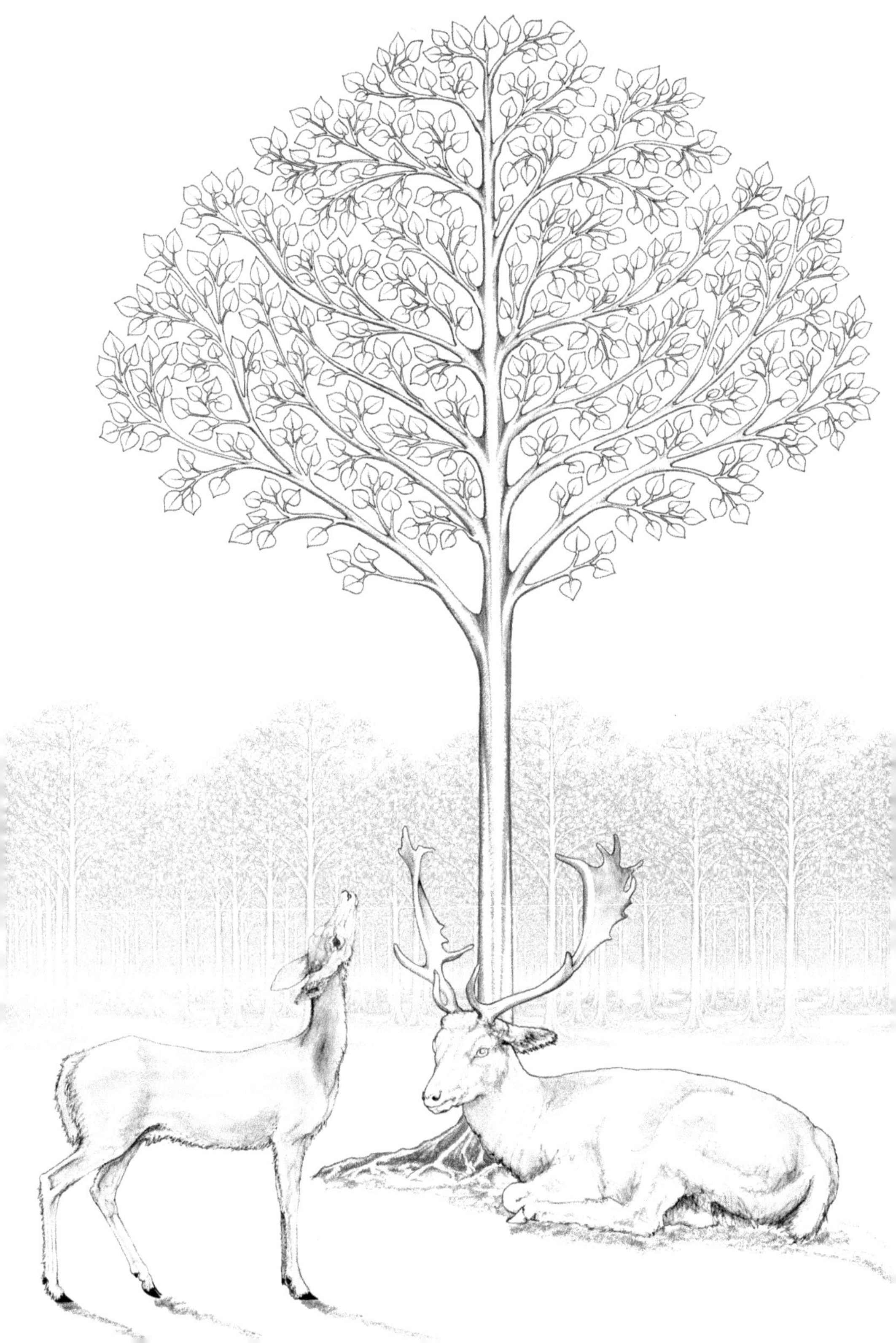

You in passing
were contained in silence,
so lightly touched the floor,
seated touched my hand.

I, all awareness
had shadows across my heart,
your tears brimming overflowed.

My thoughts circling
are held by memory.

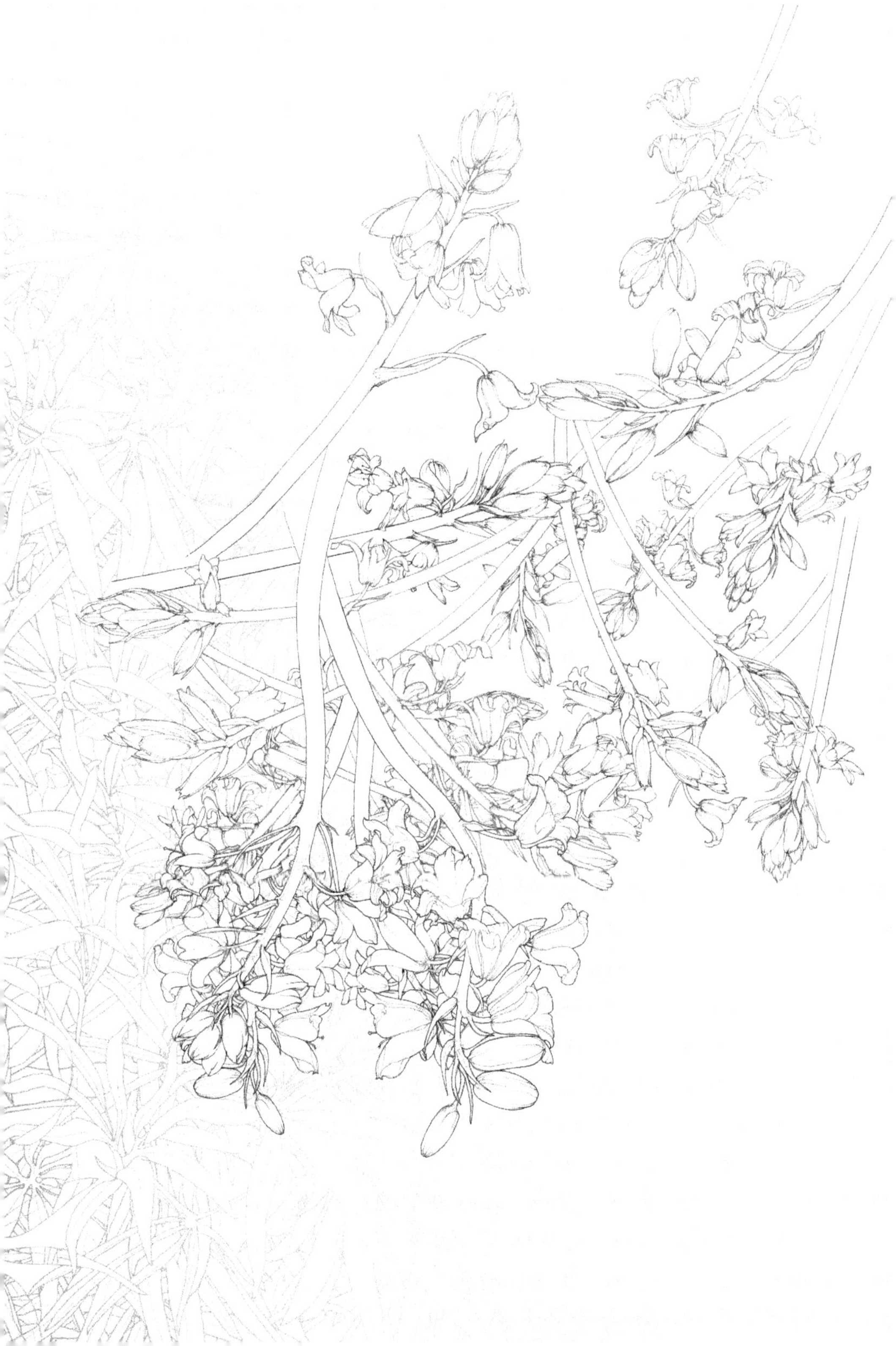

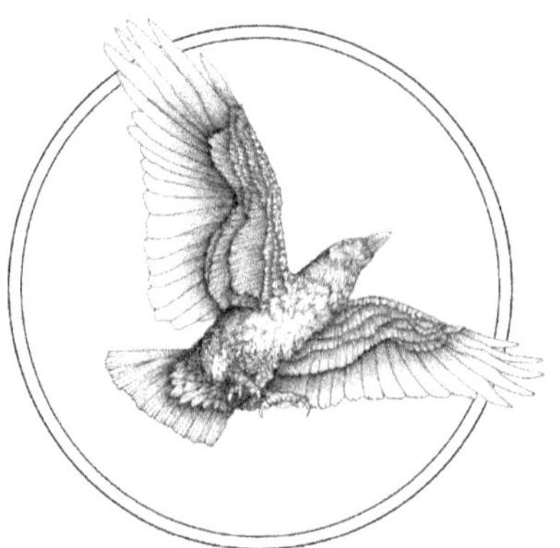

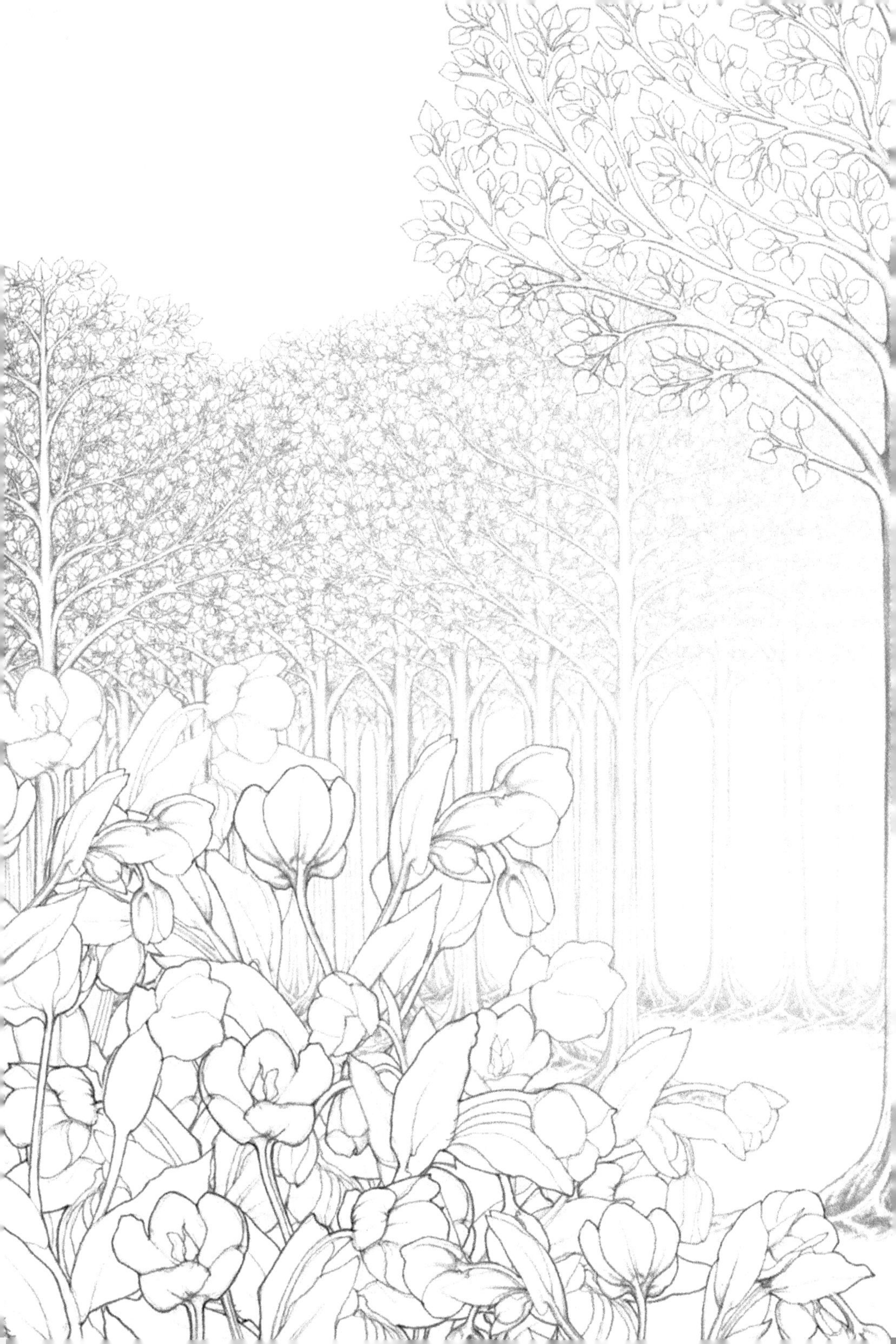

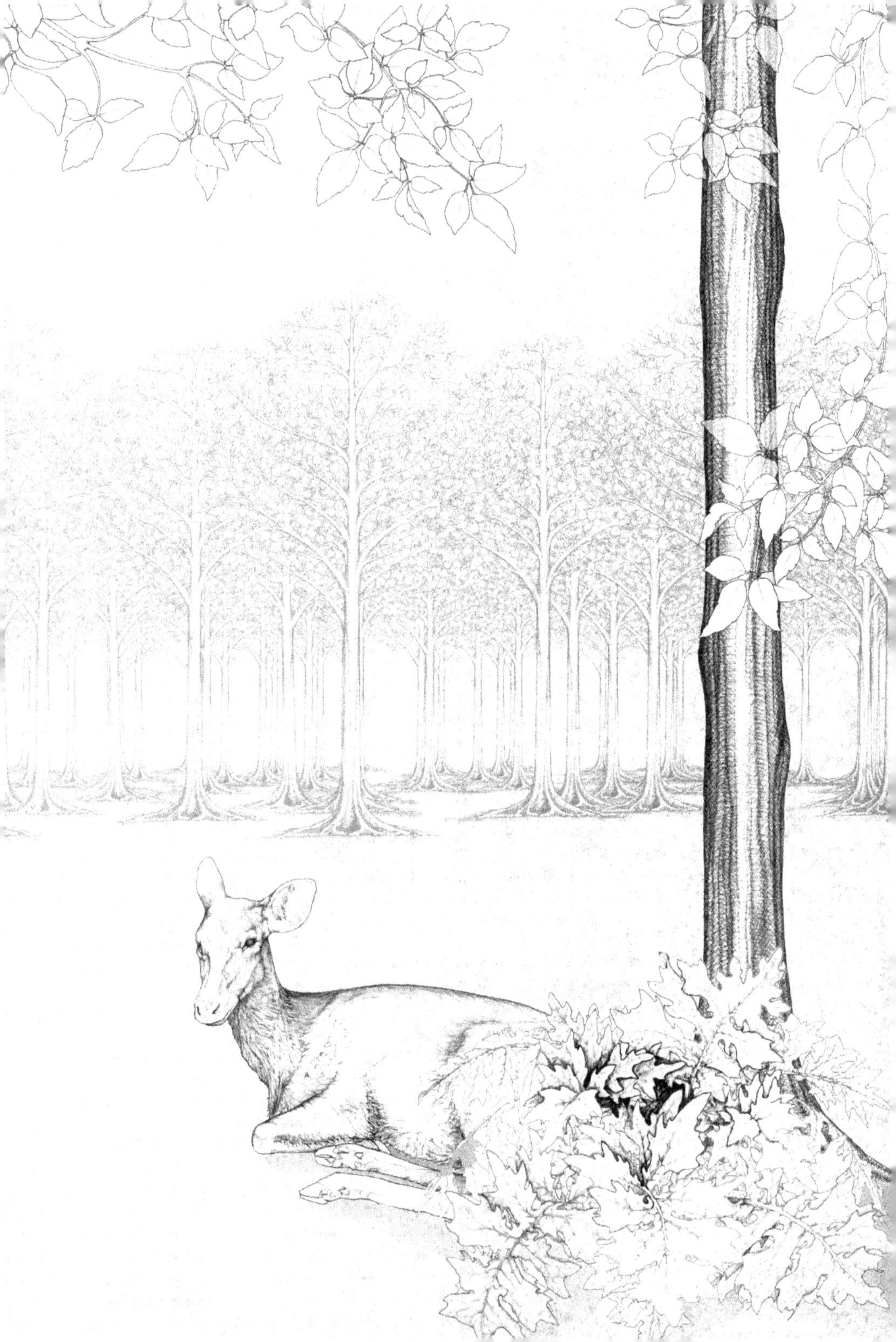

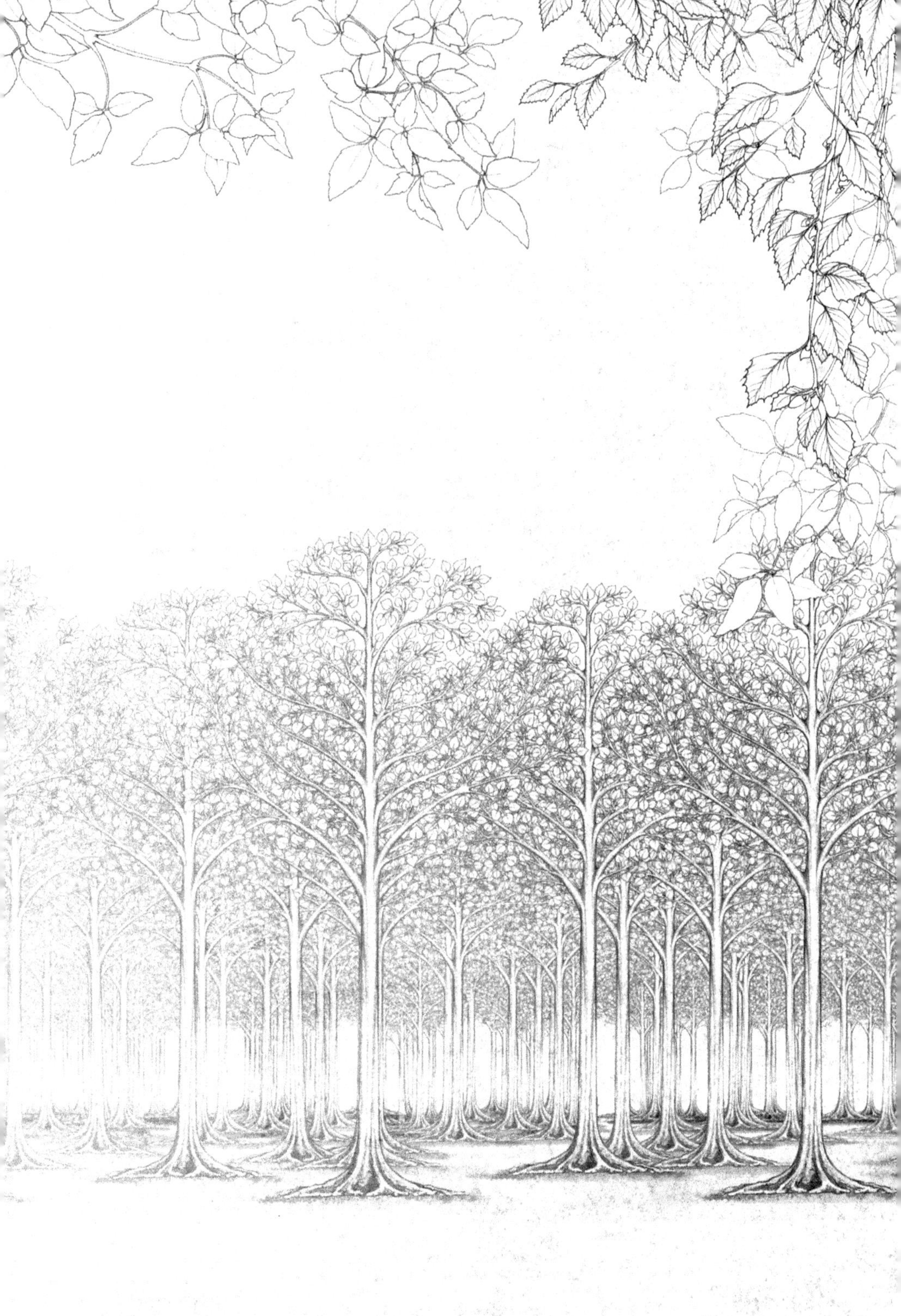

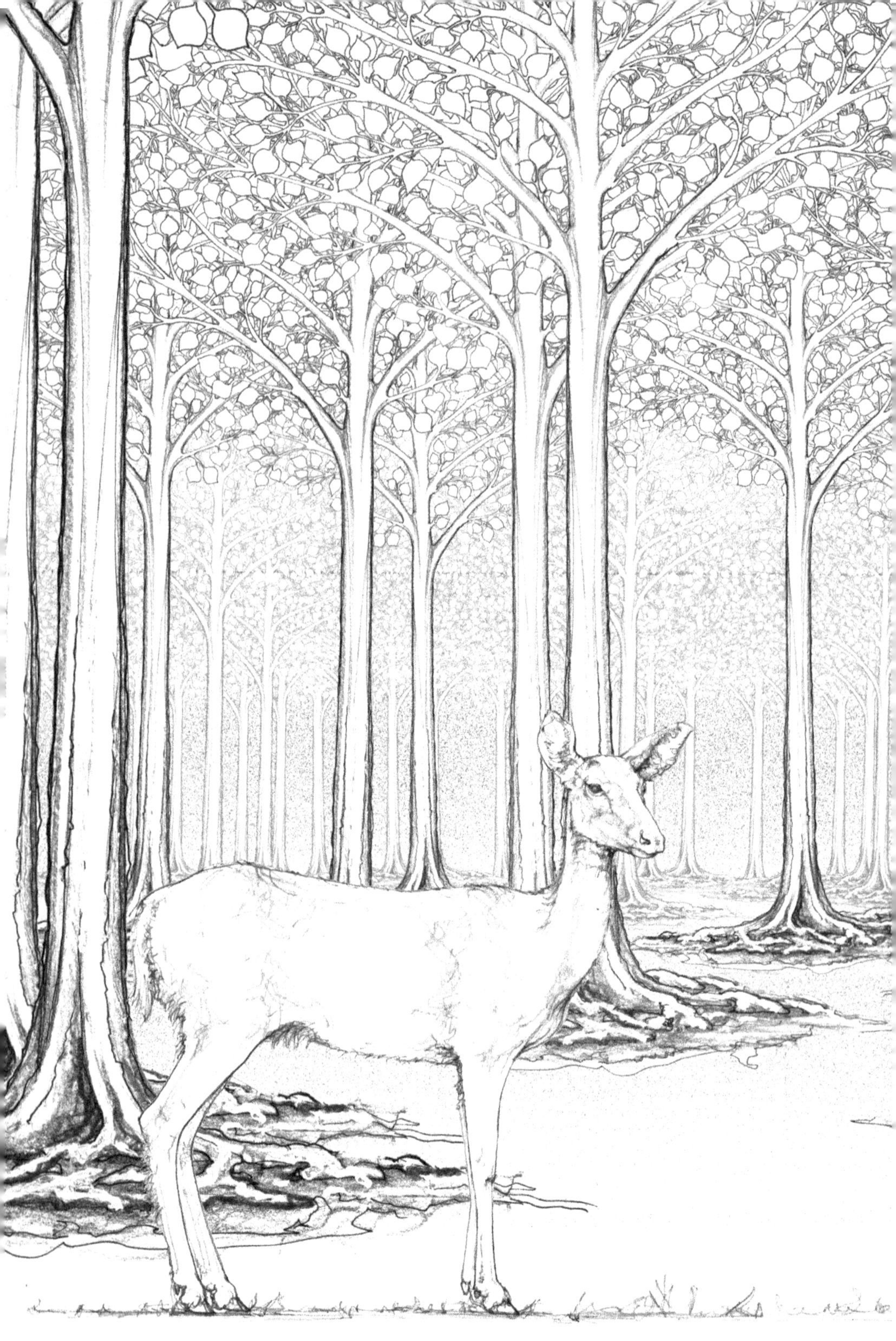

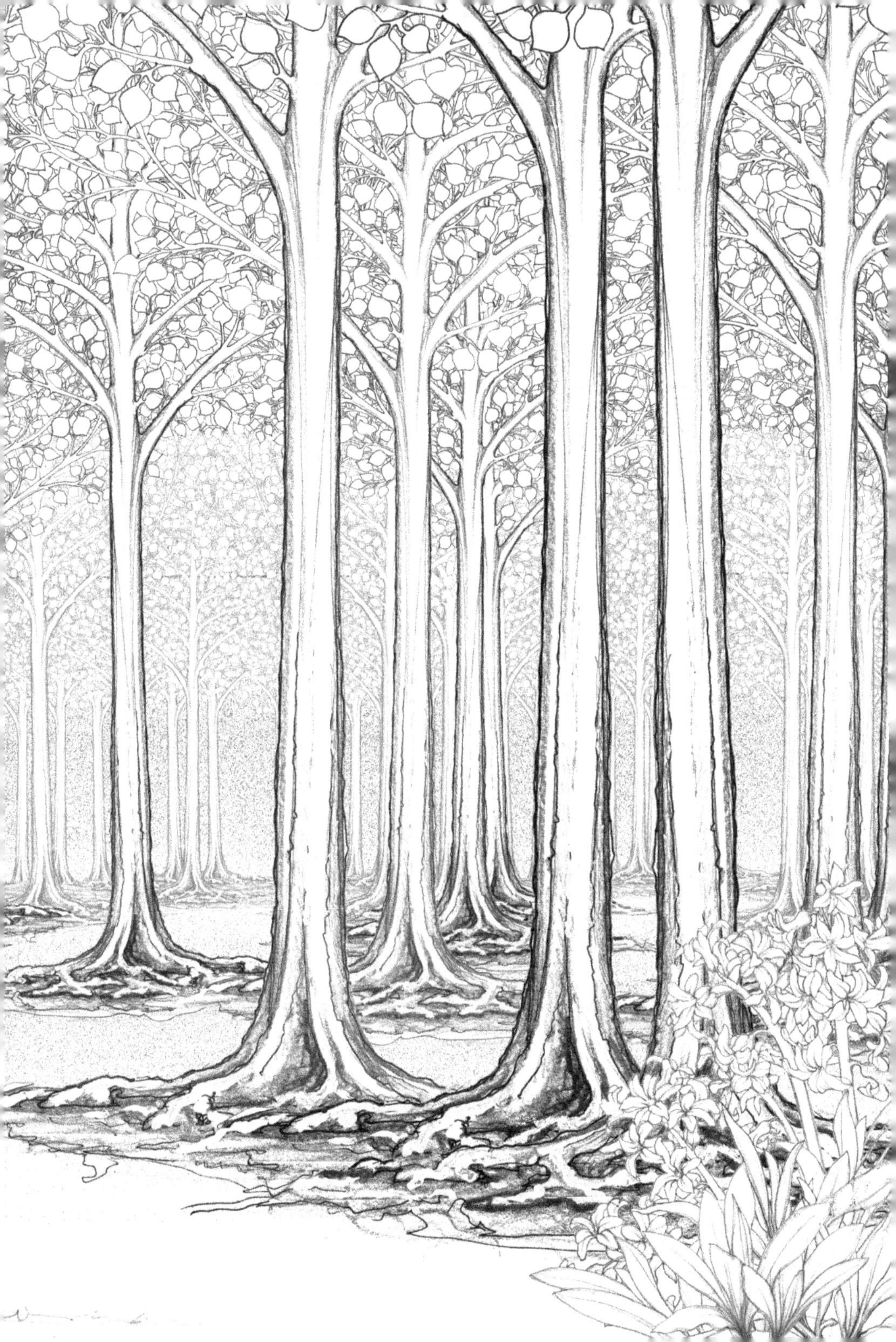

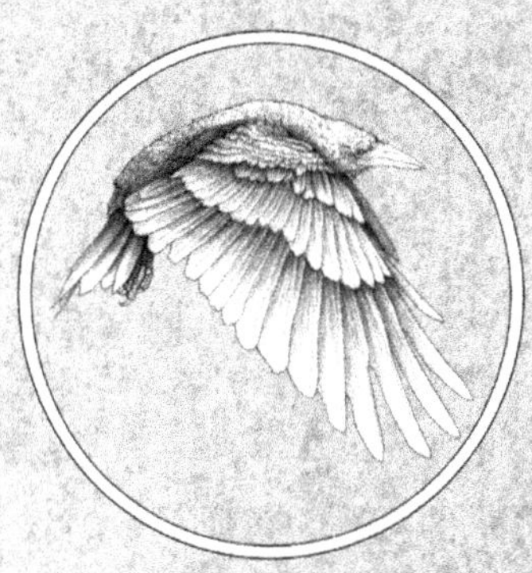

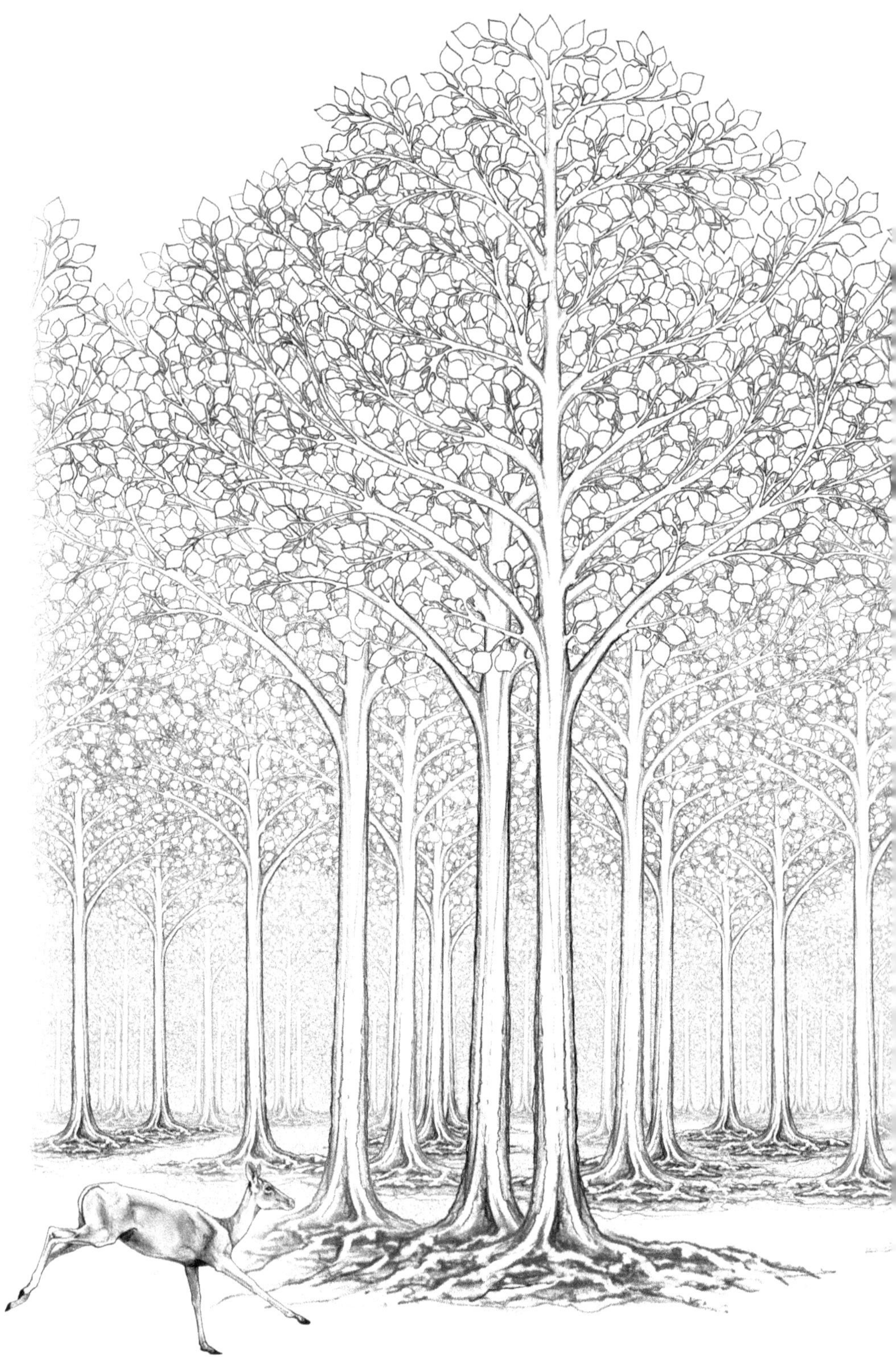

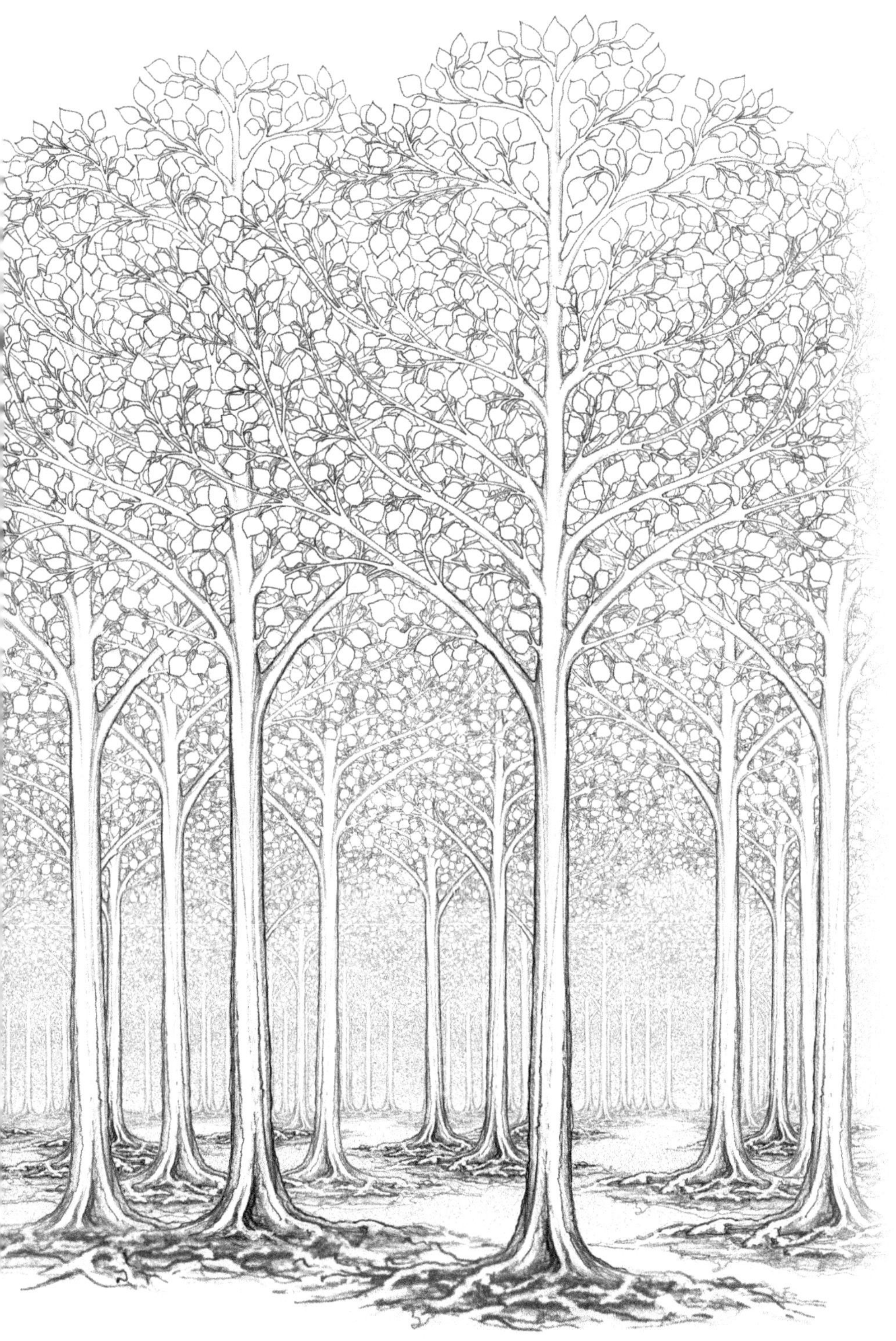

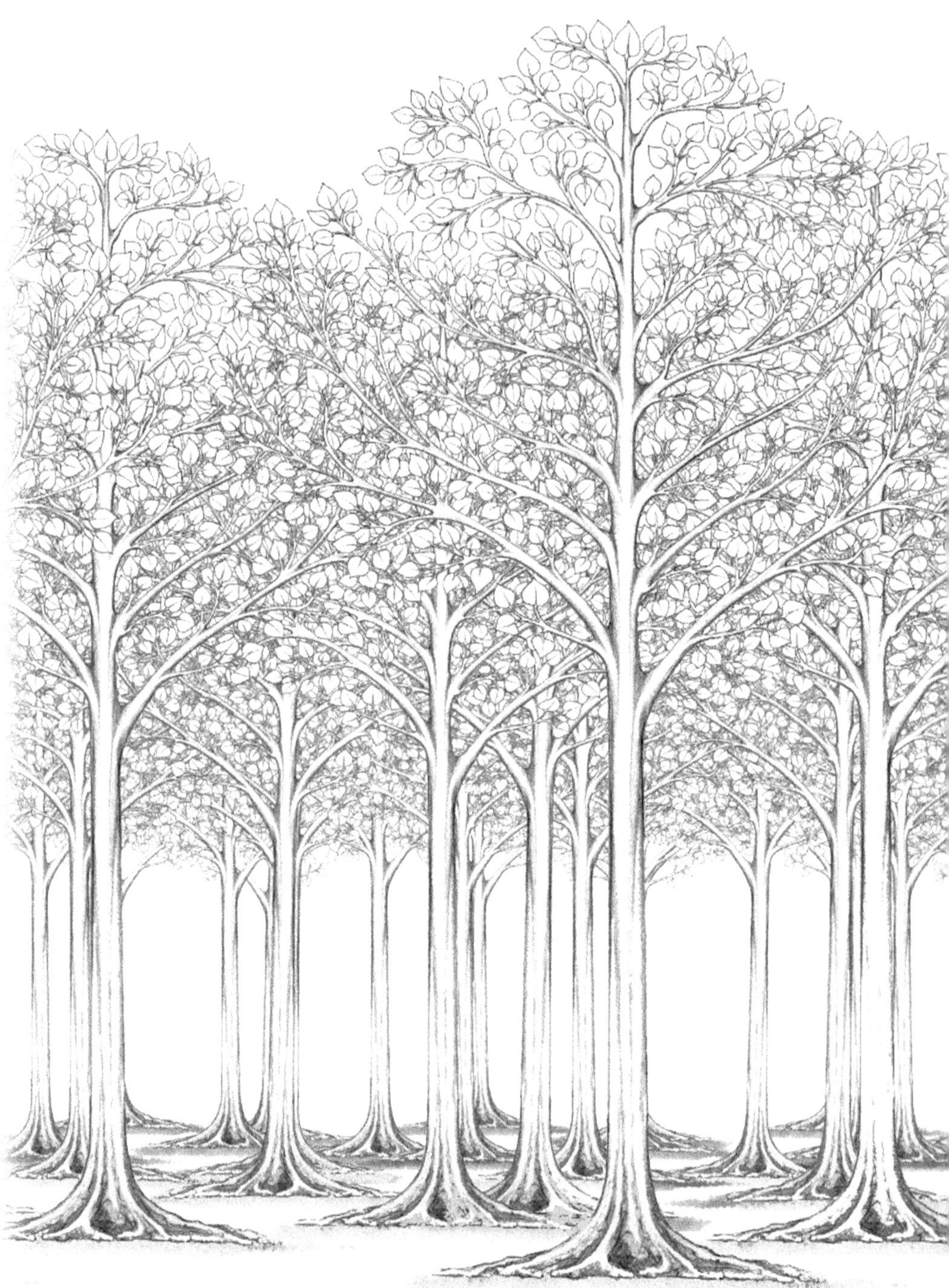

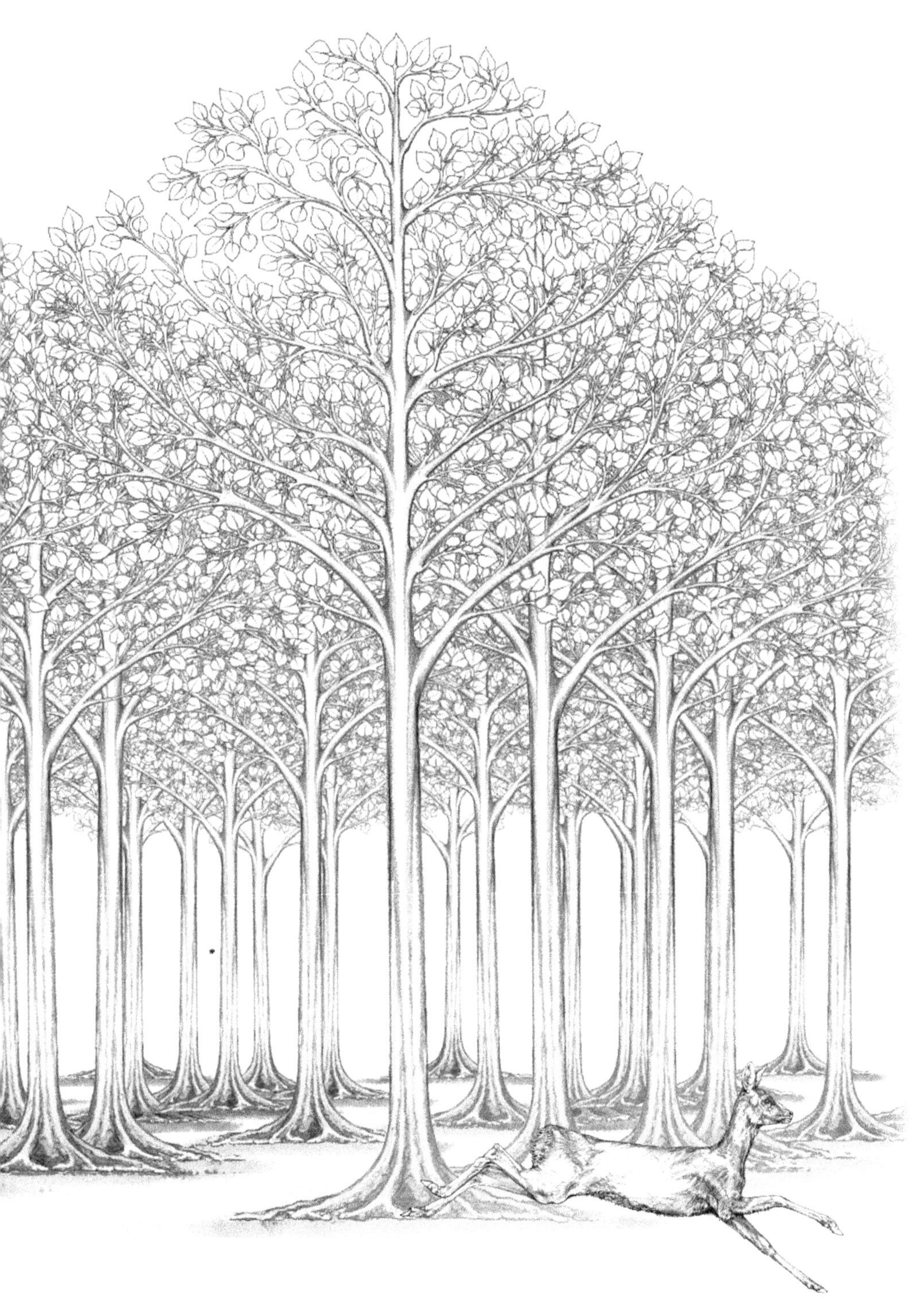

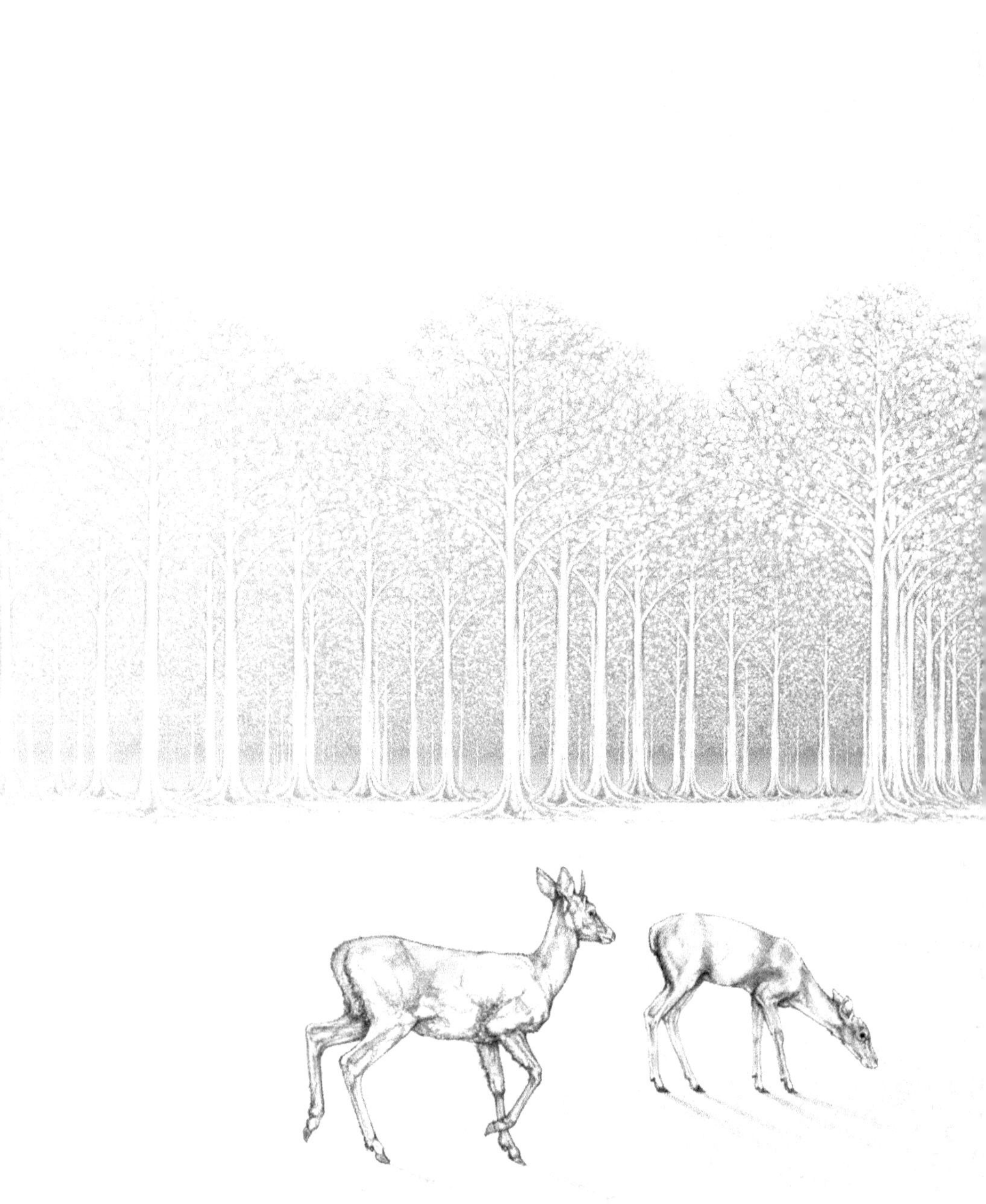

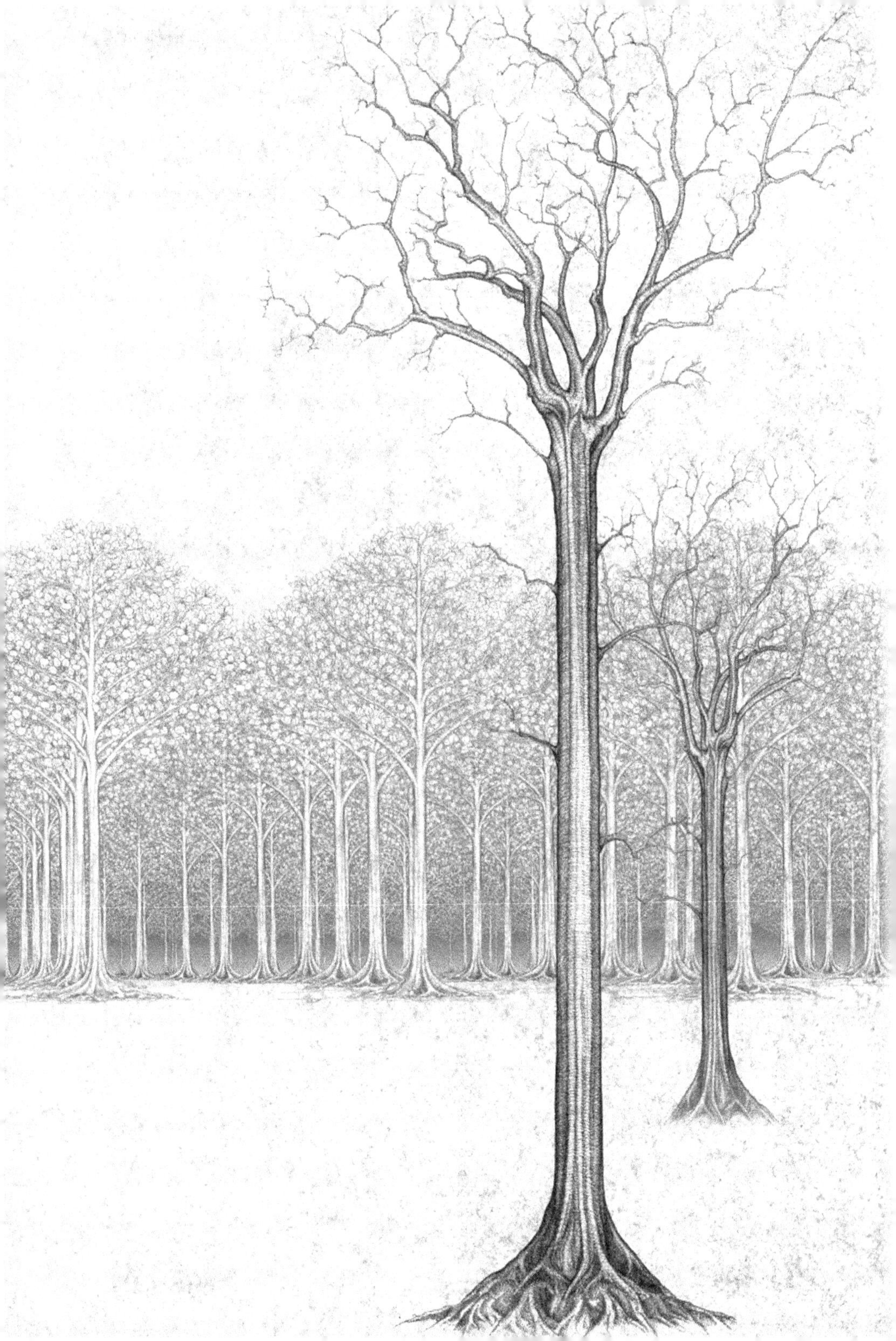

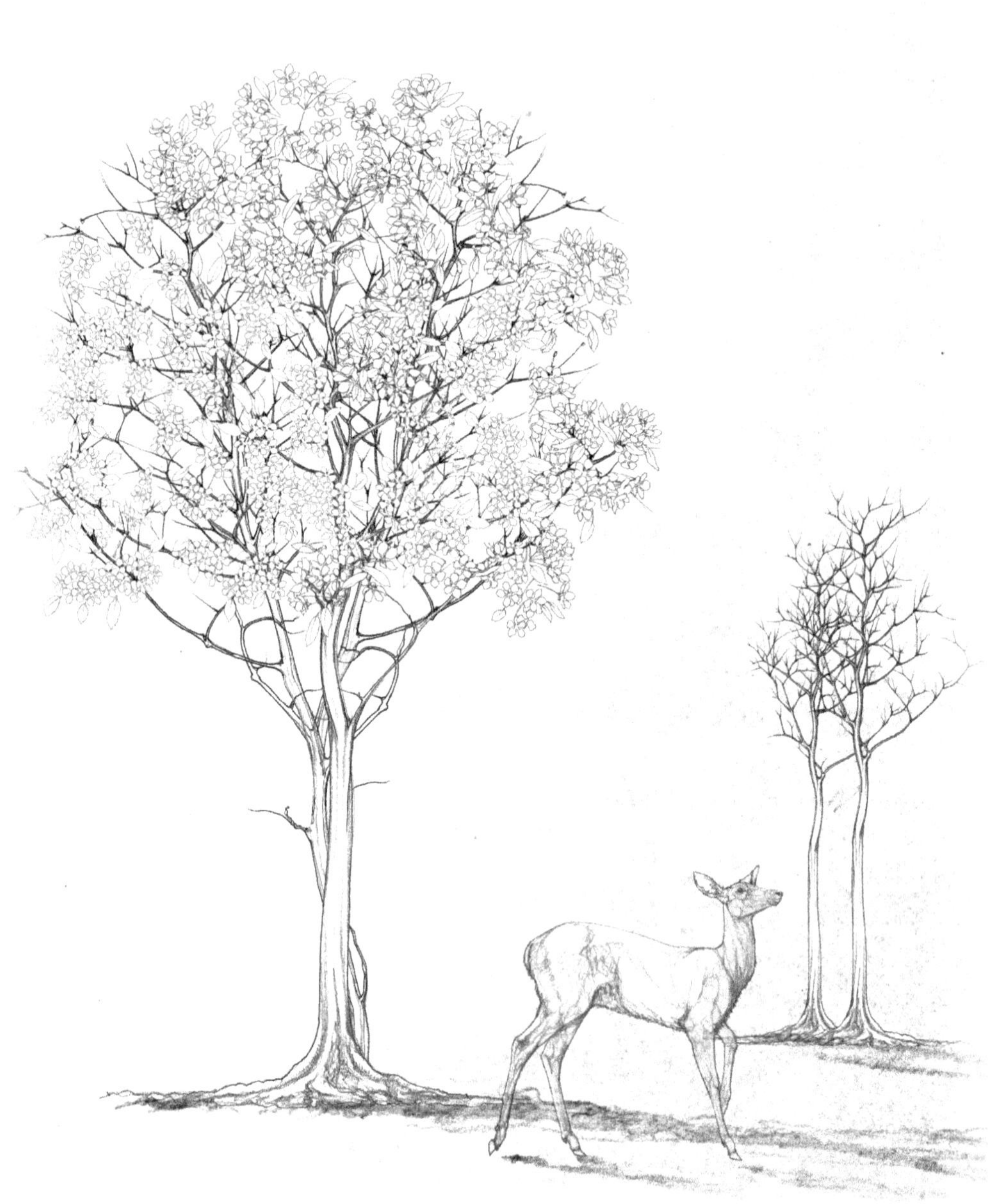

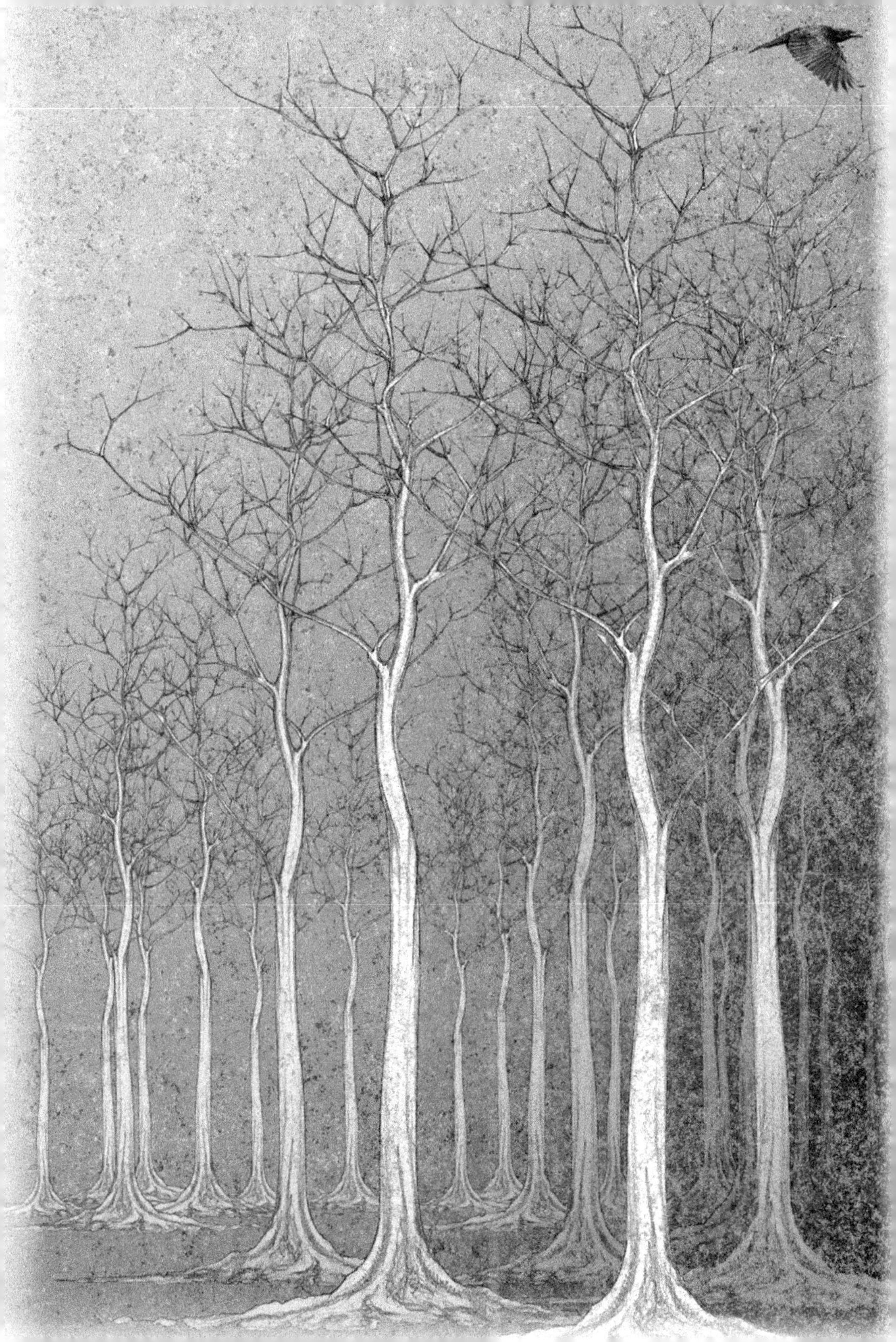

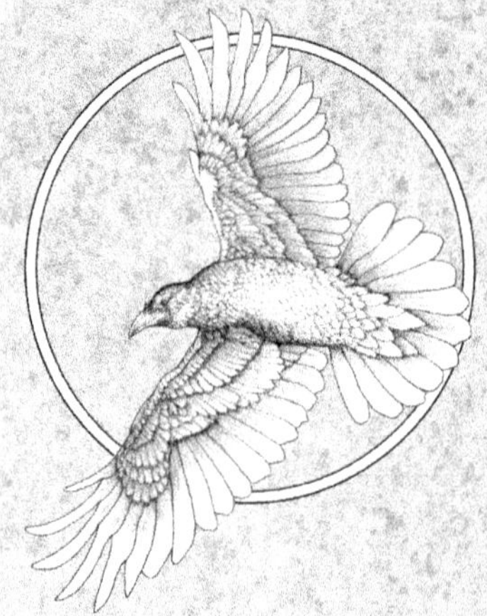

Our footsteps leave no trace
there is no way back.
Each step precarious falters
where once we ran secure.
The solid ground dissolves,
beneath our feet are
dim and tangled shadows,
in our minds confusion.
Each passing face
a mirror and a question.
You seem integrated, whole,
I a shell
in which a restless flux,
mere smoke,
is filled with ghosts.

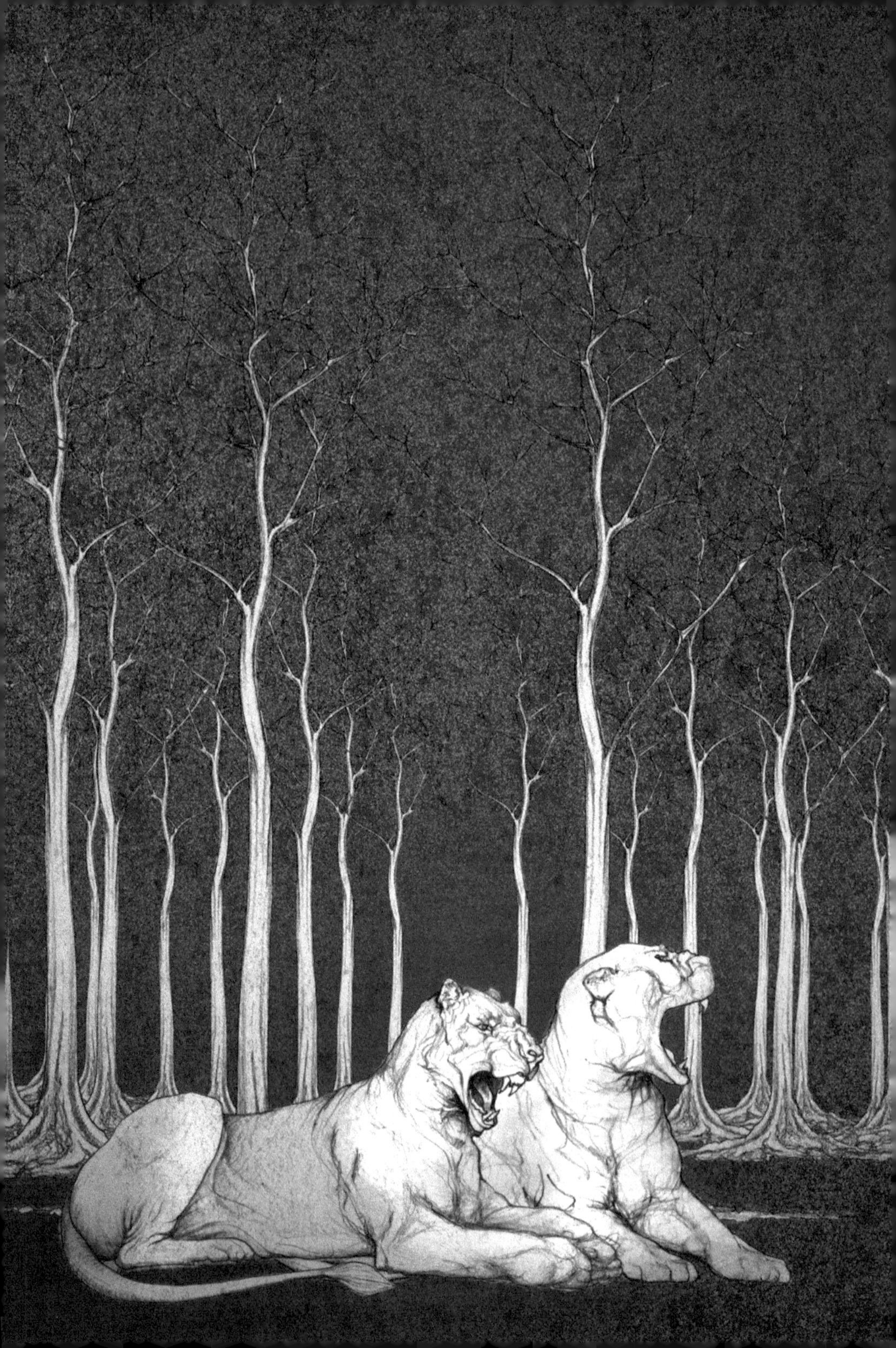

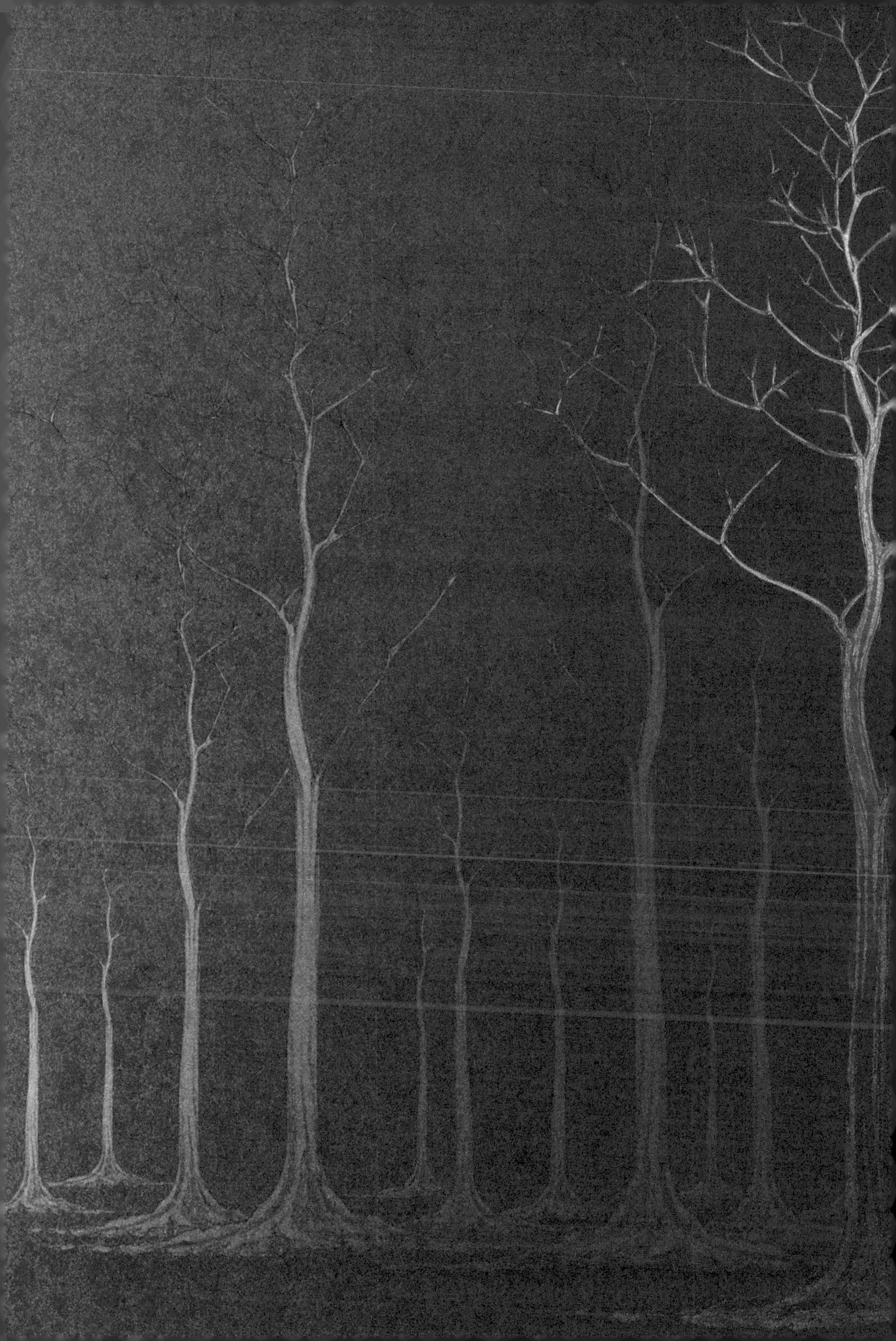

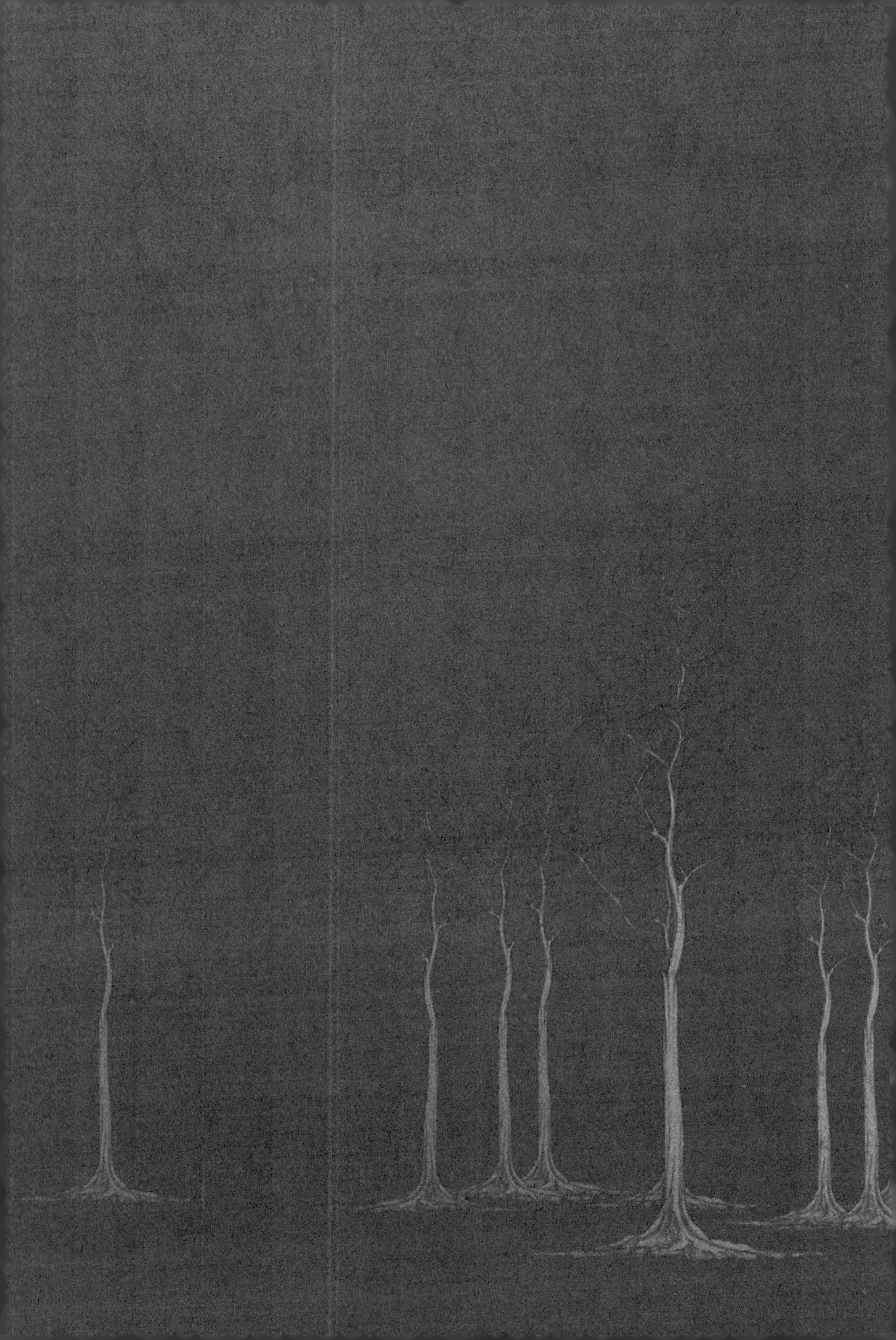

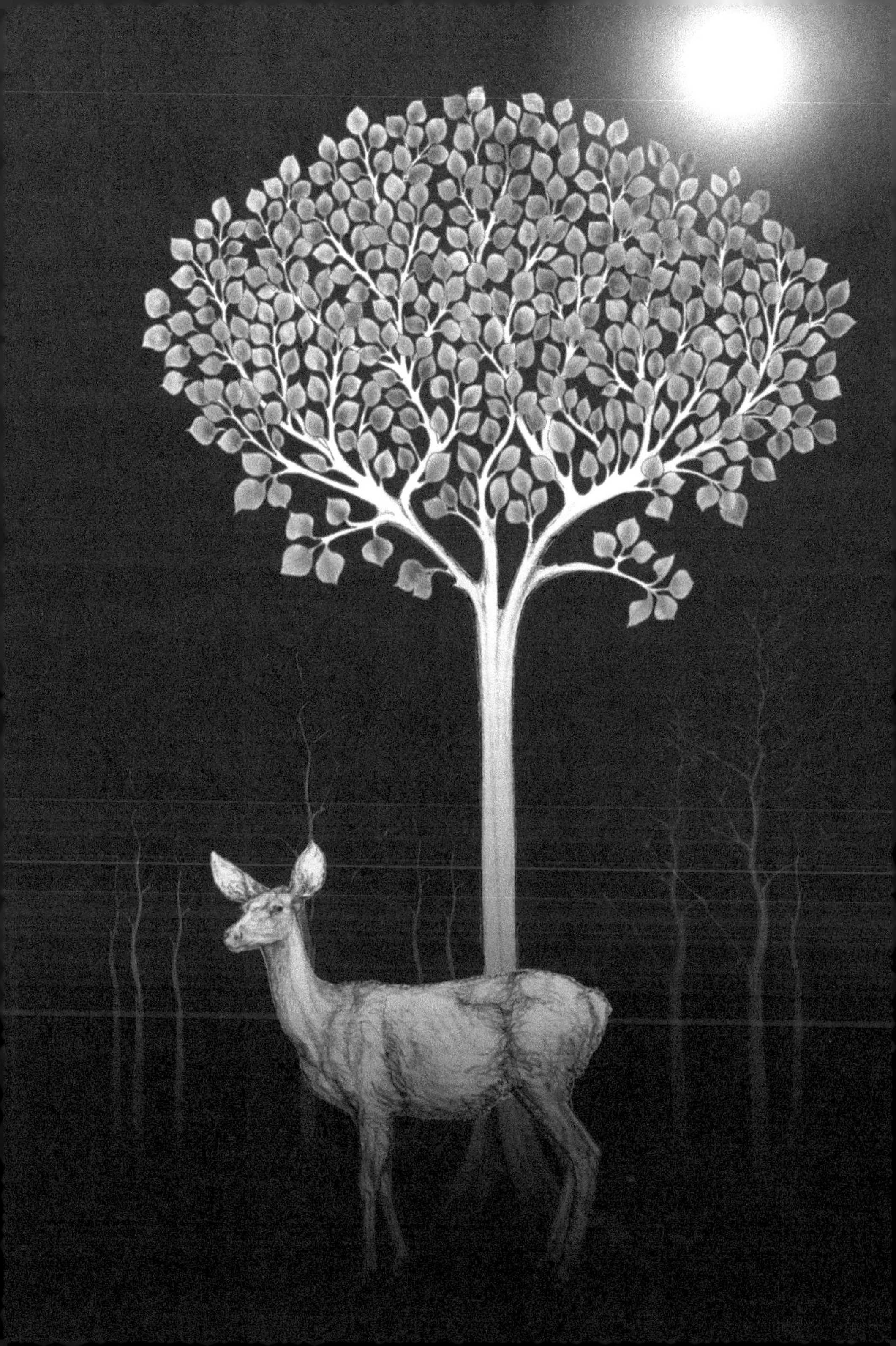

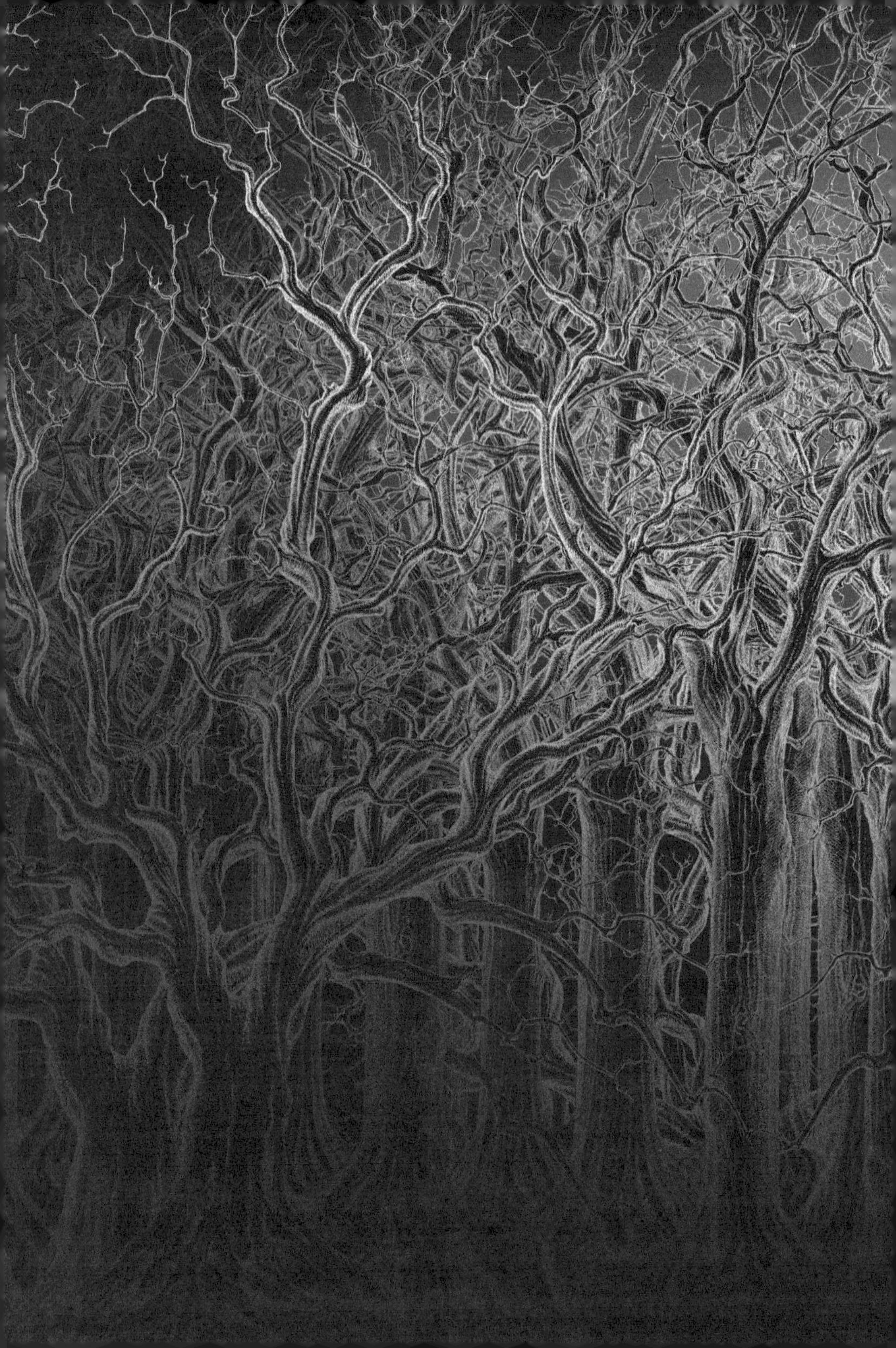

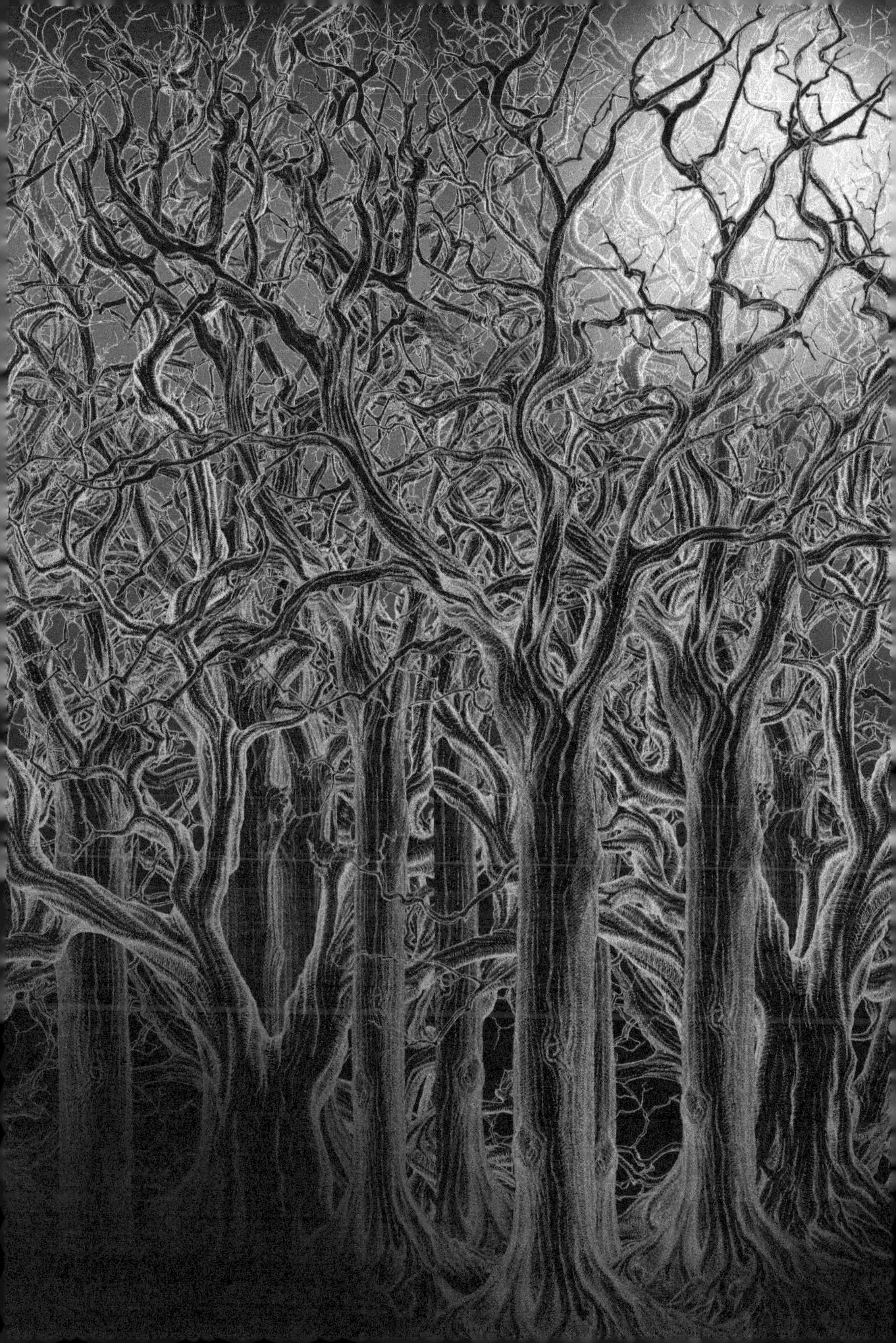

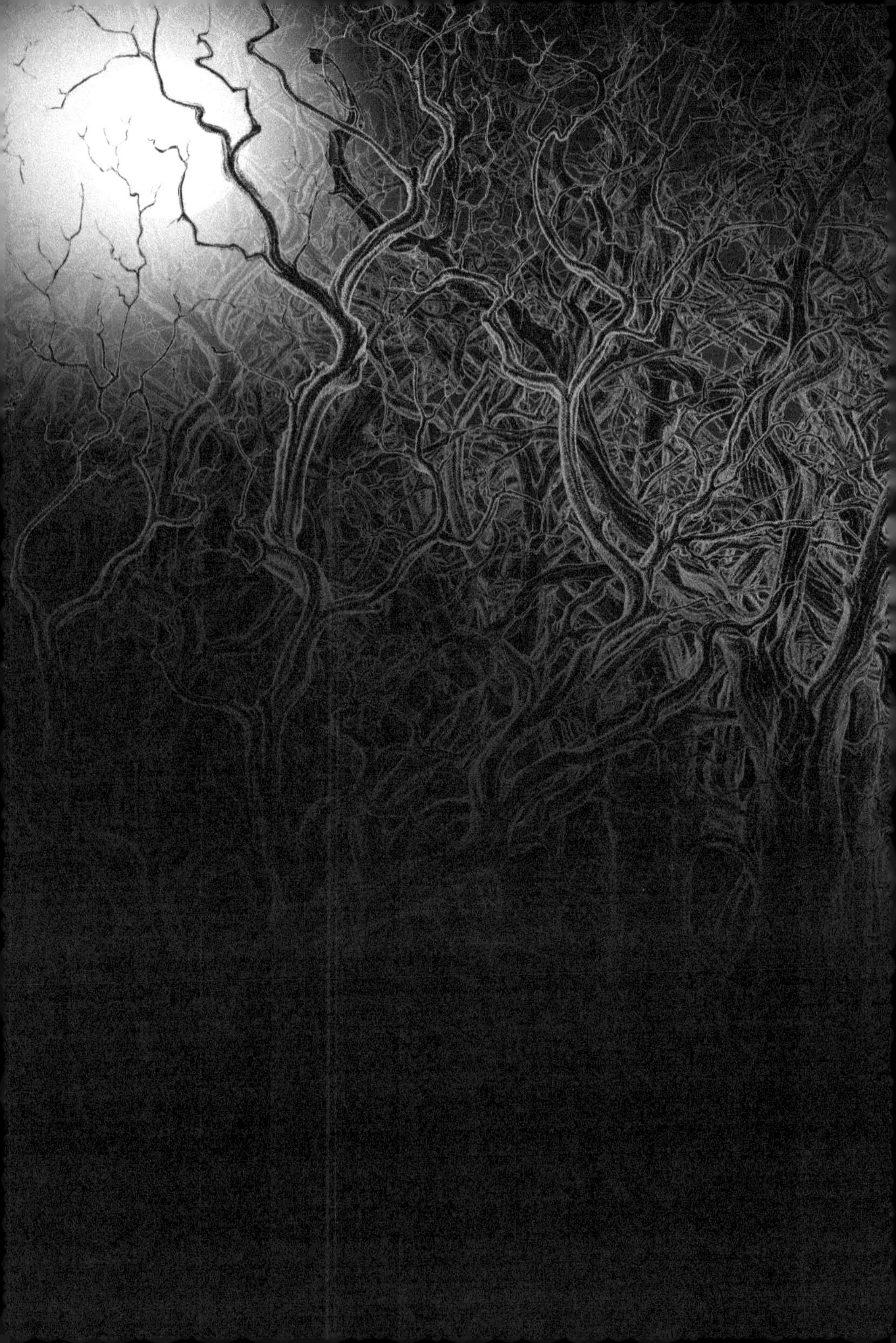

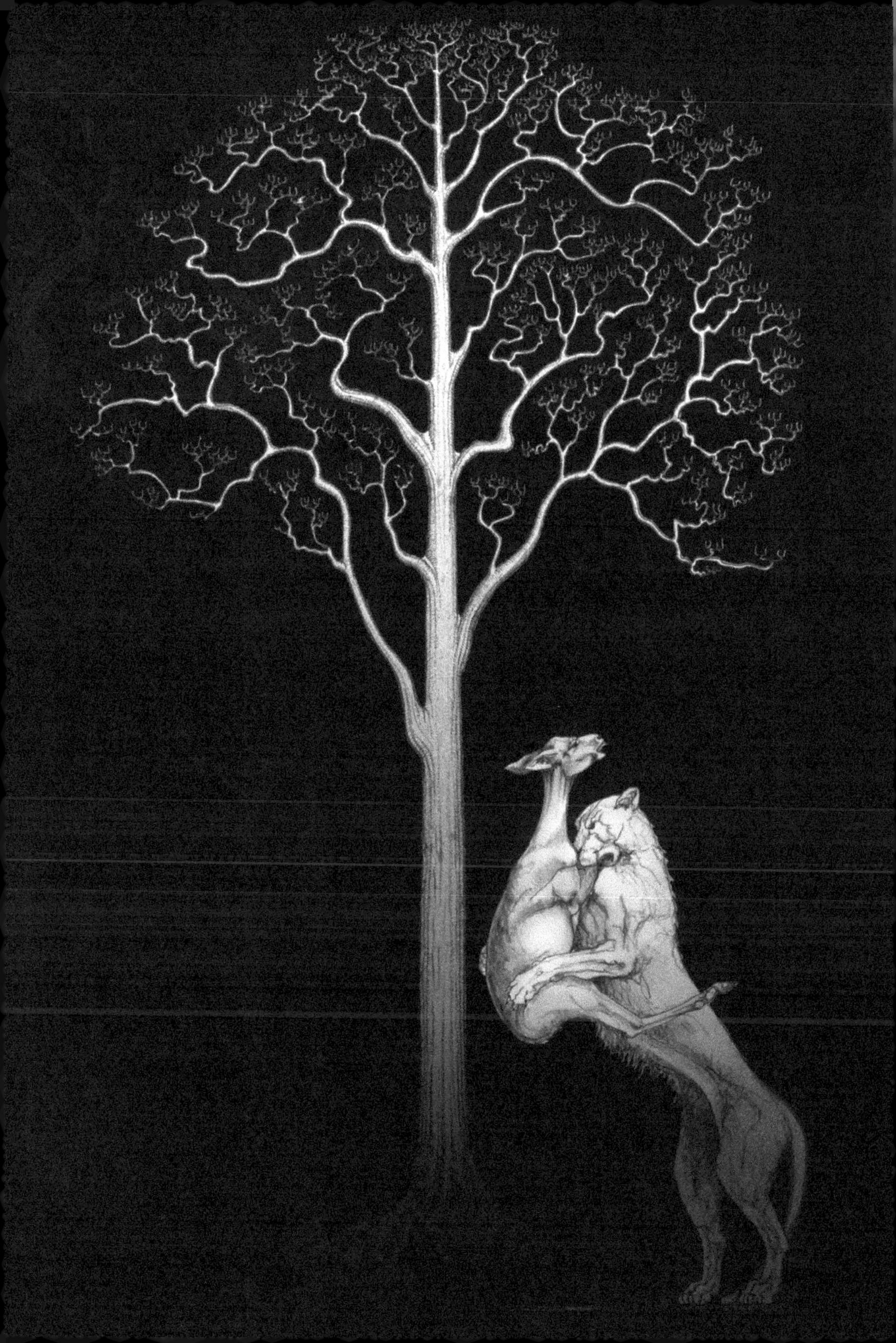

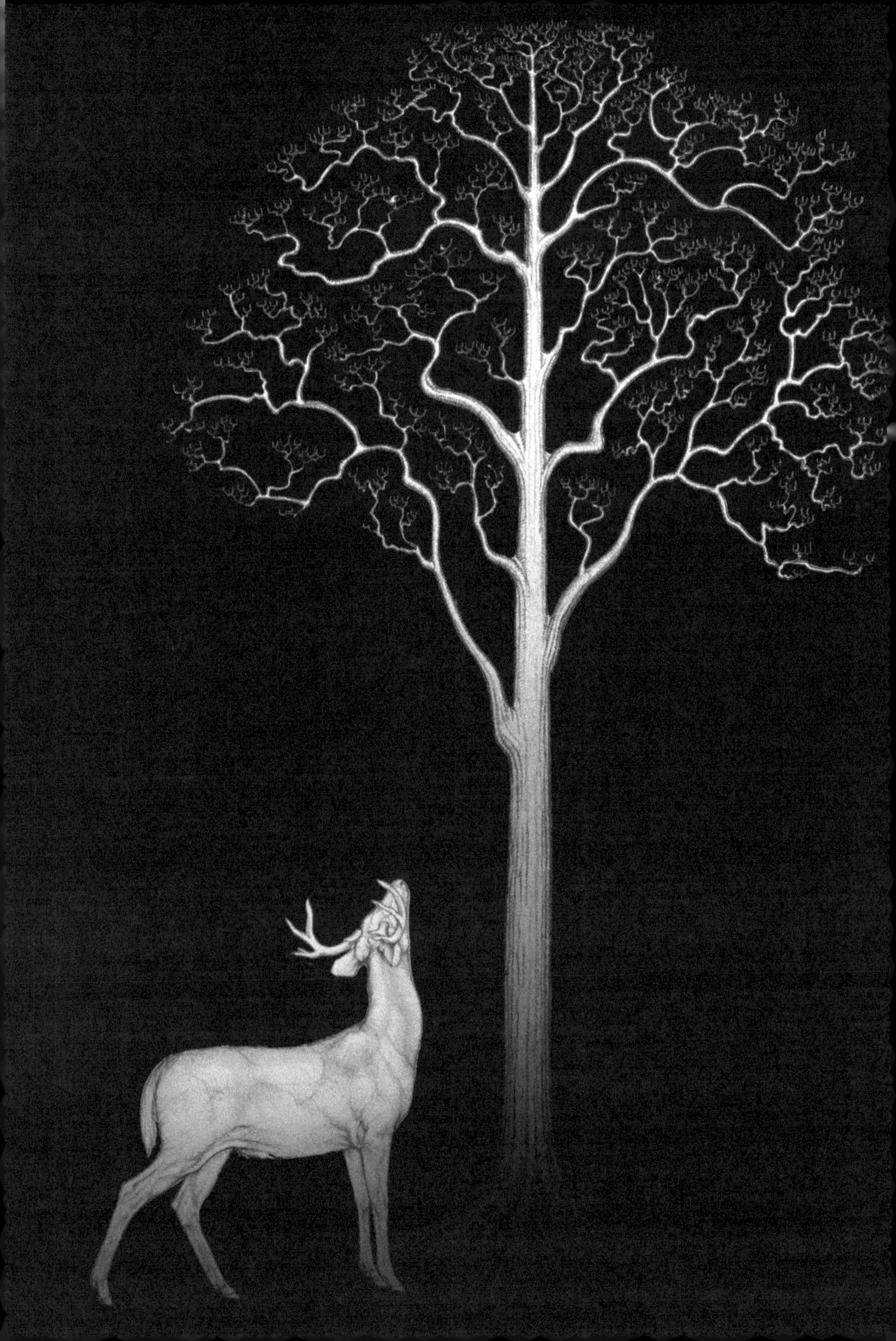

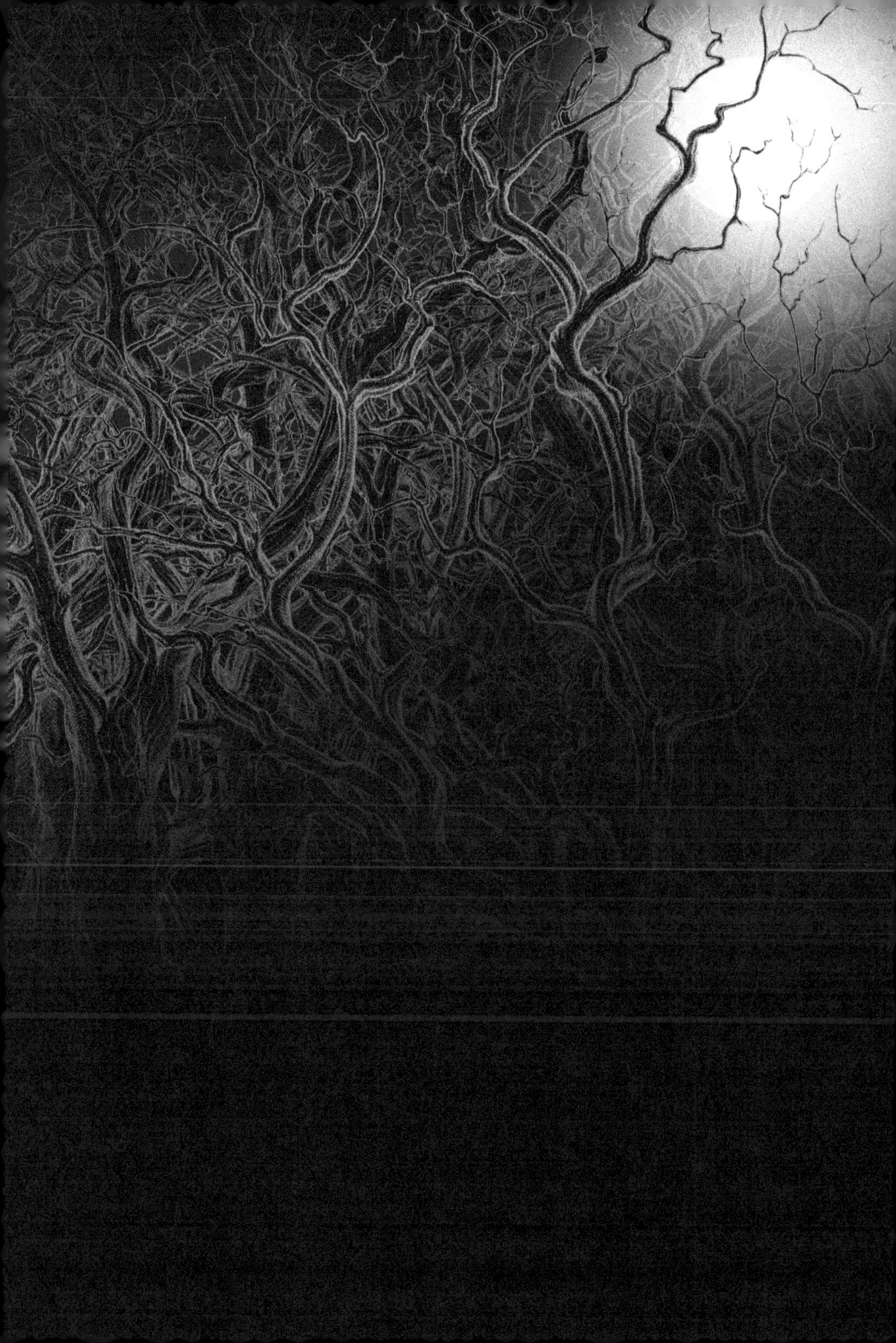

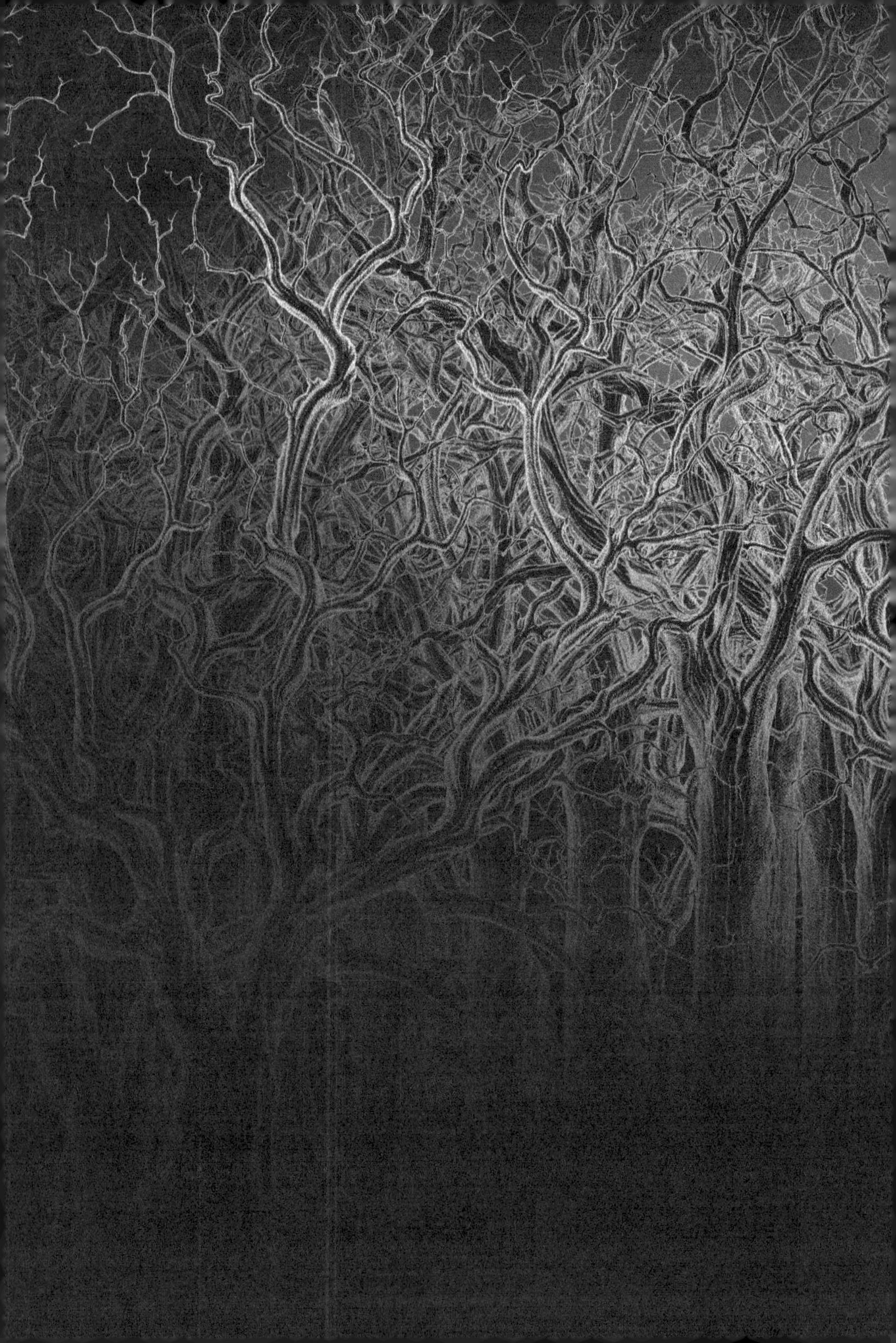

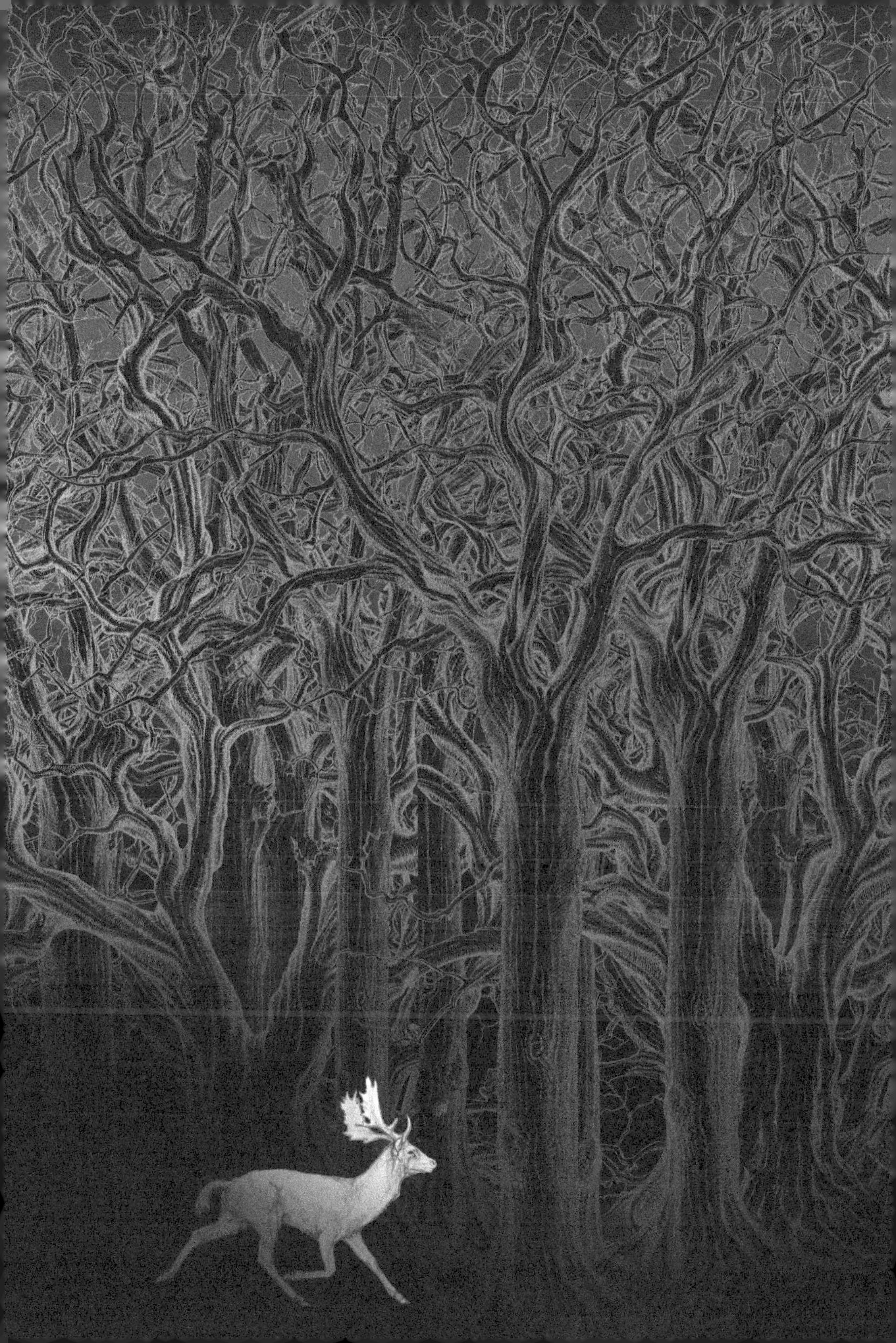

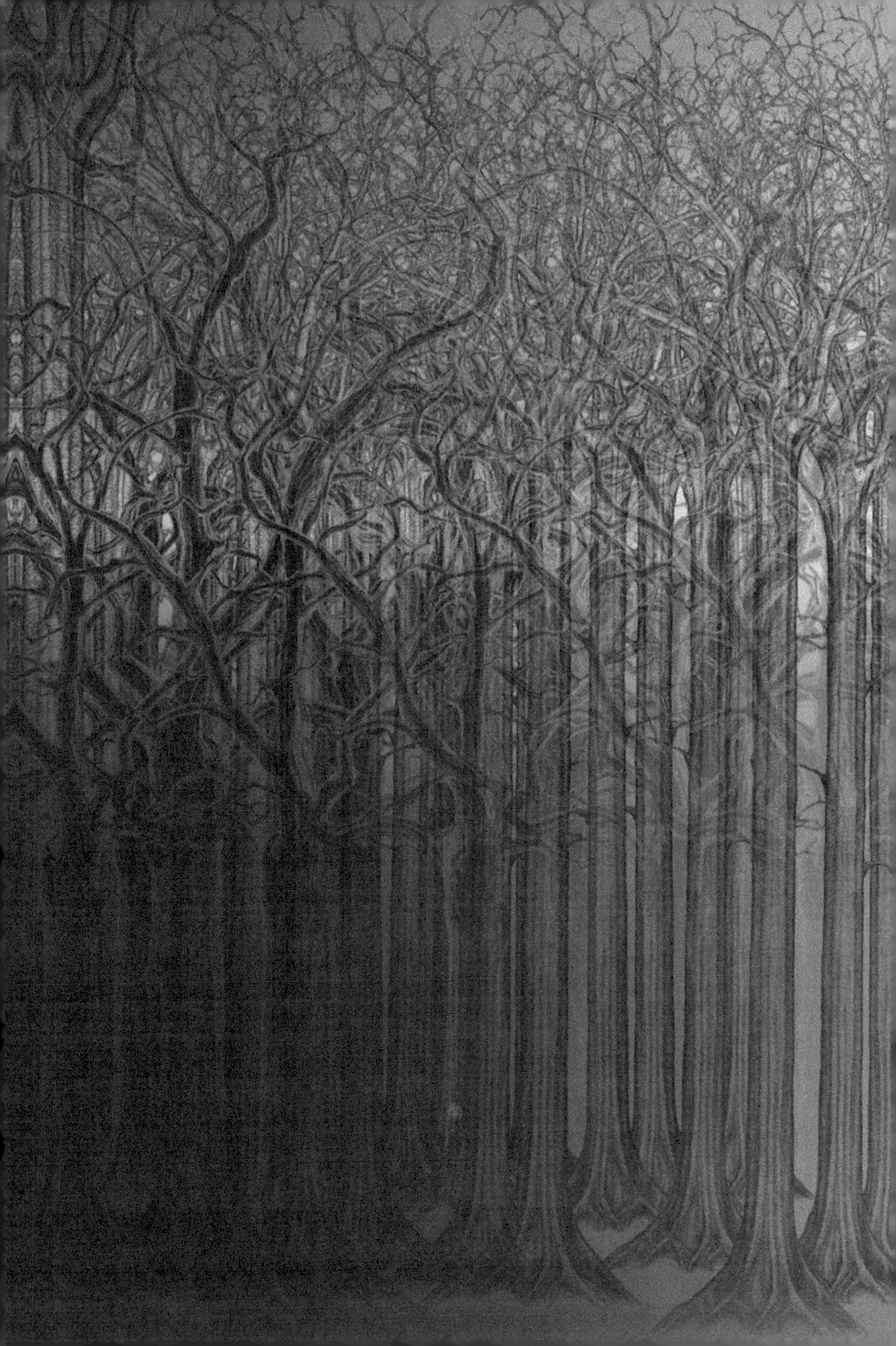

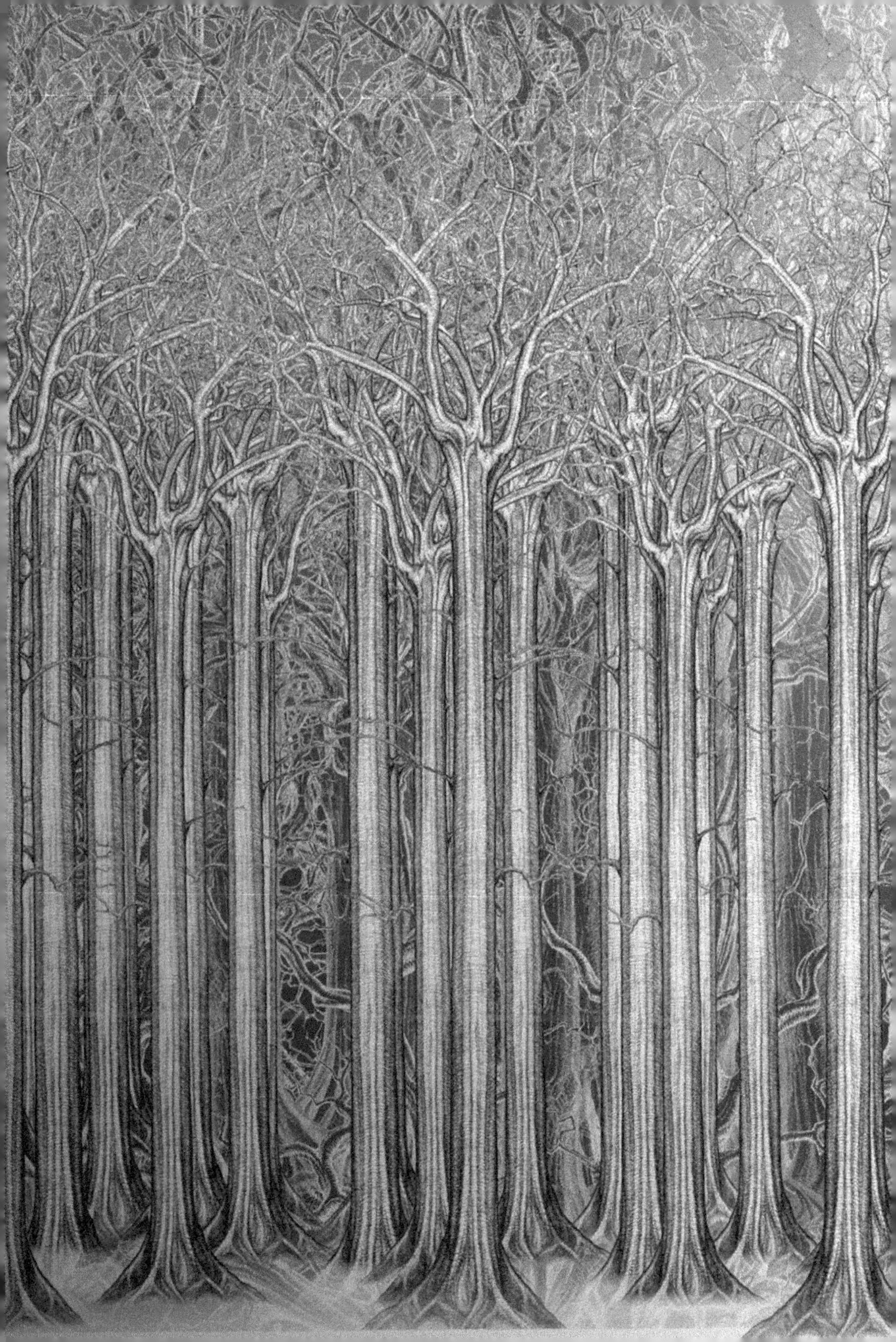

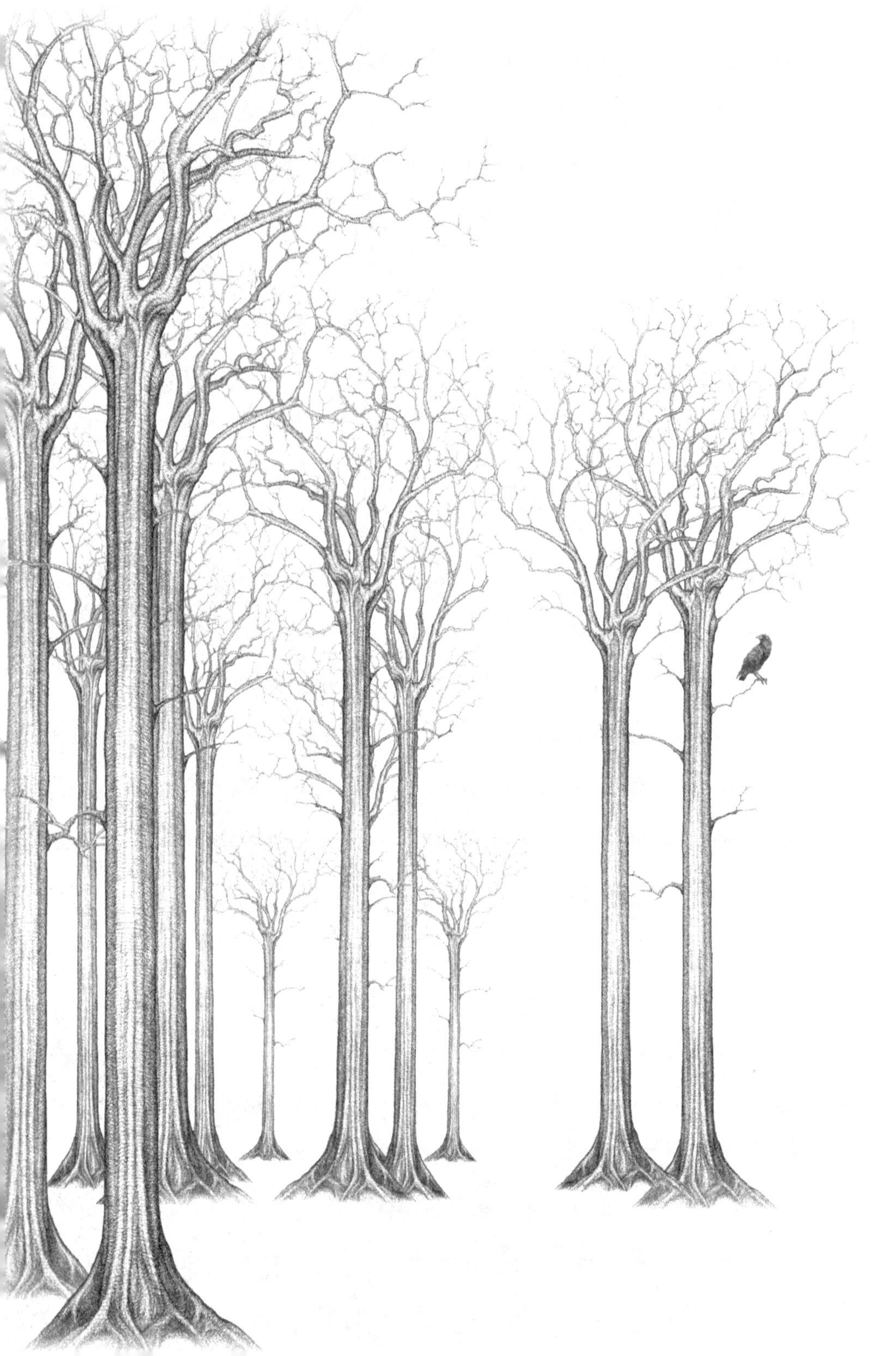

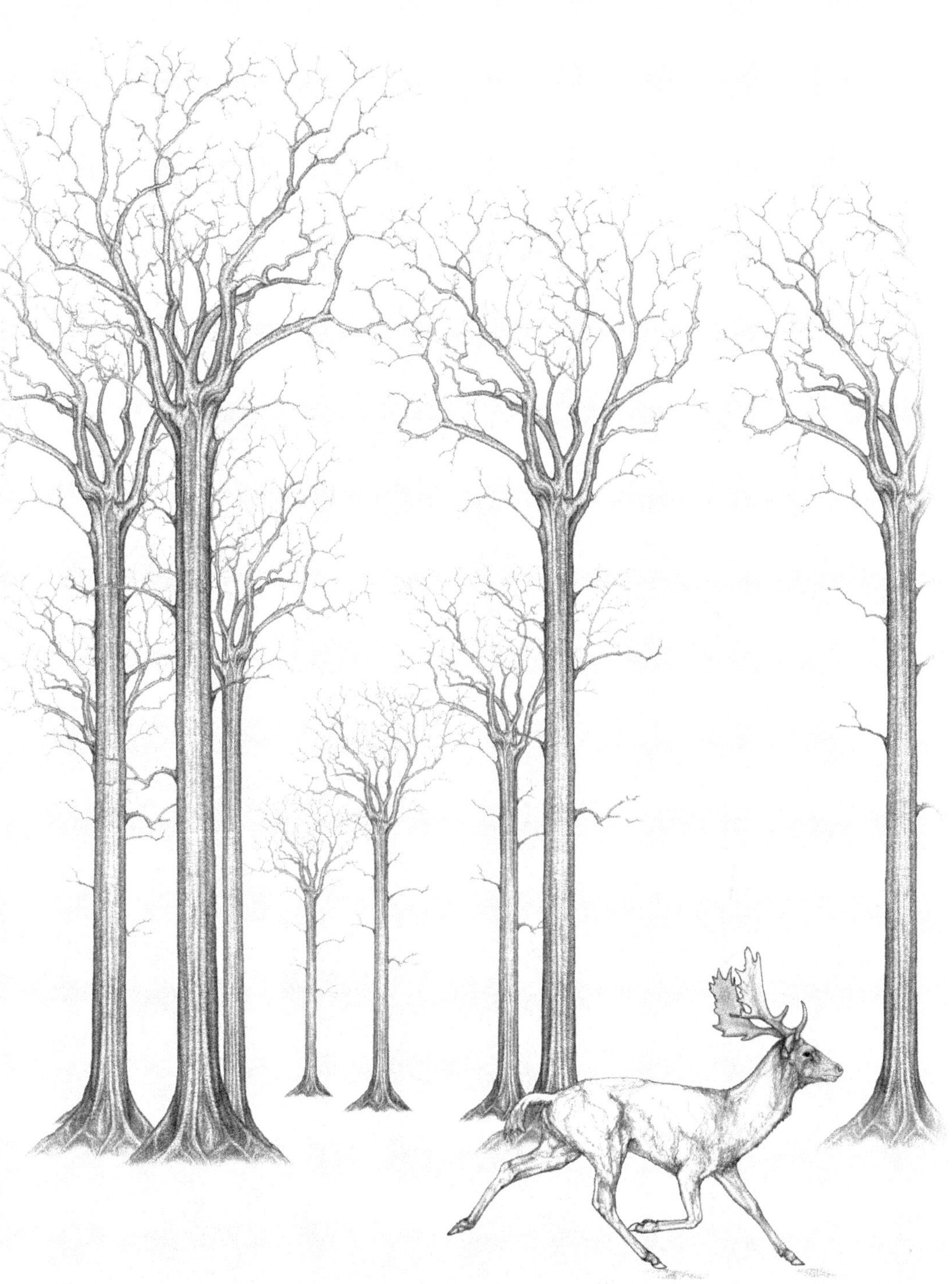

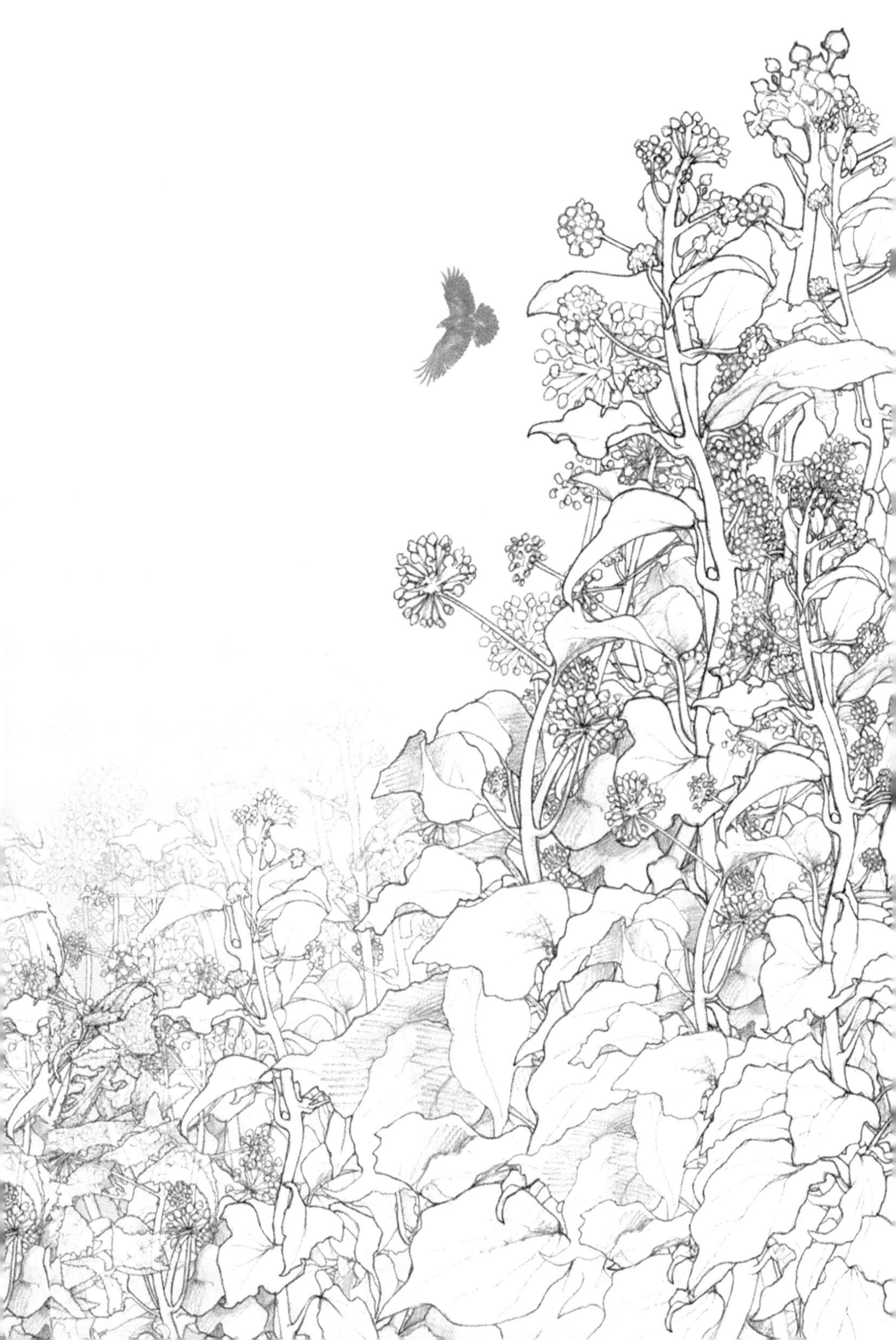

Held in this high room
for the duration of my life,
from these high windows to view
the sunlit world.
Within thoughts circle
coalesce in vaporous forms,
divide, dissolve, re-form
Sometimes I doubt
my own reality
in this concealing hollowness.

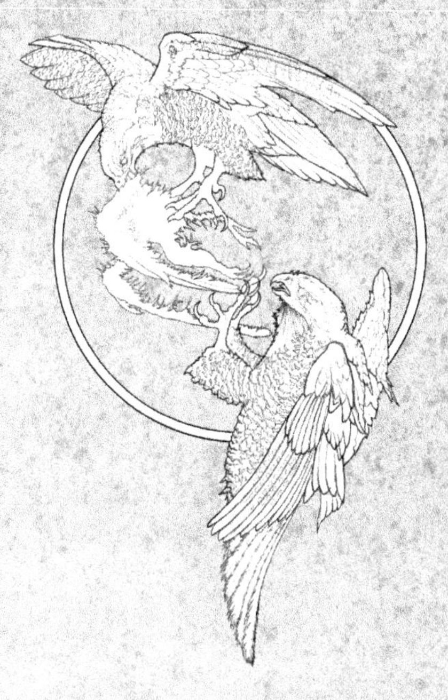

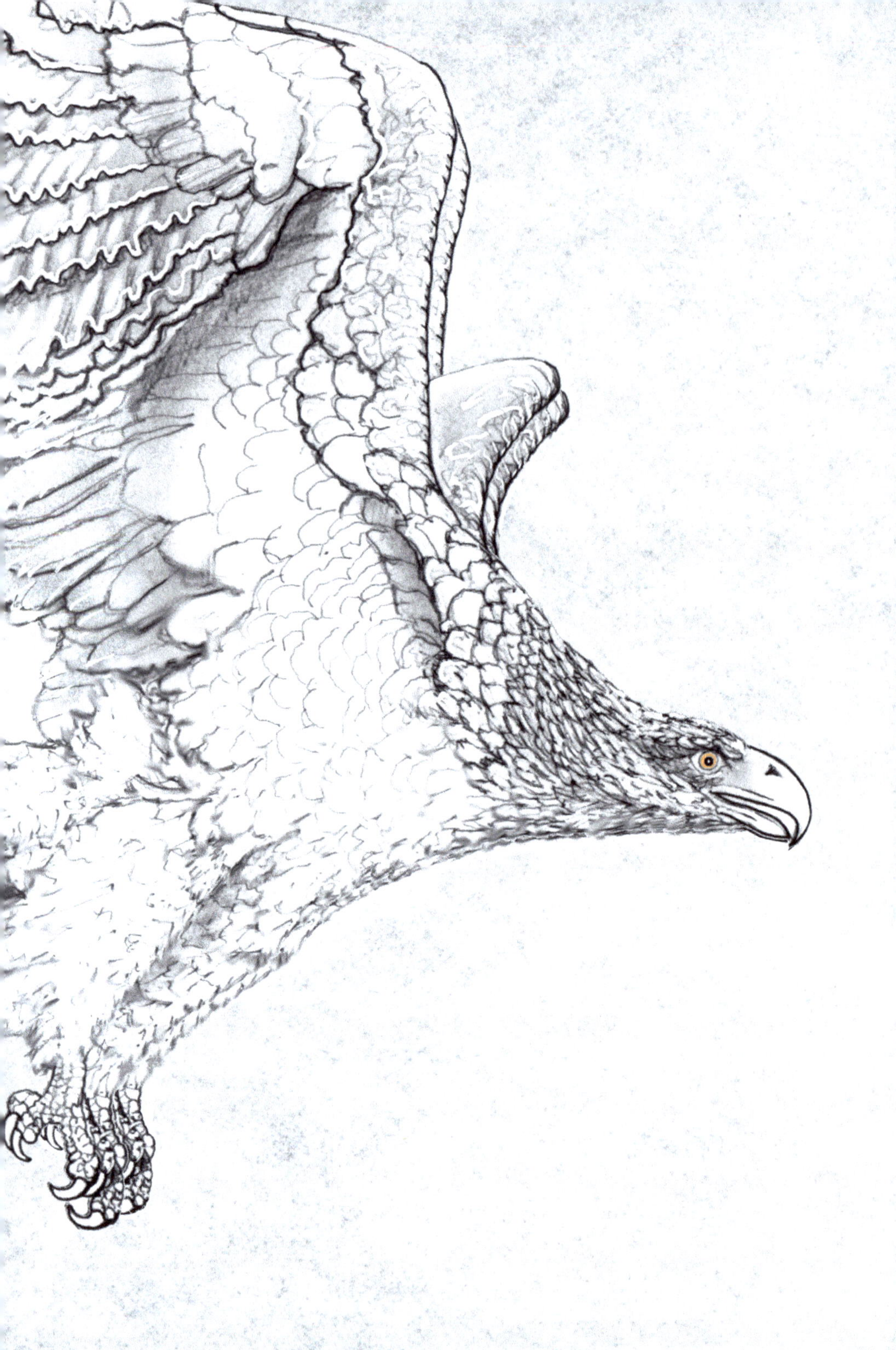

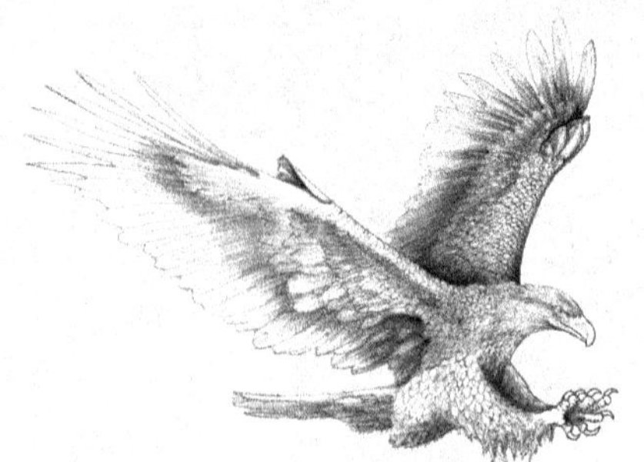

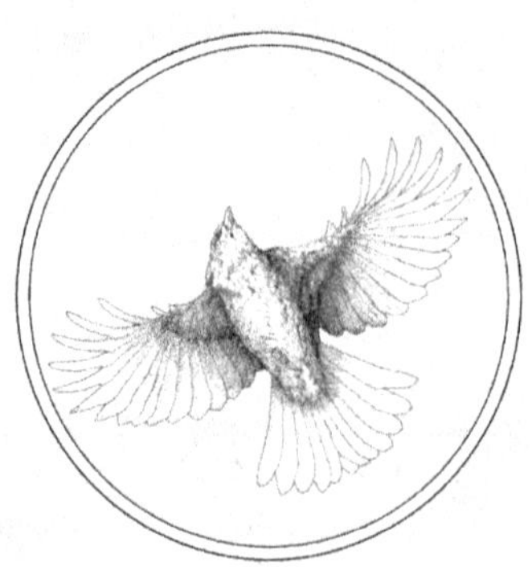

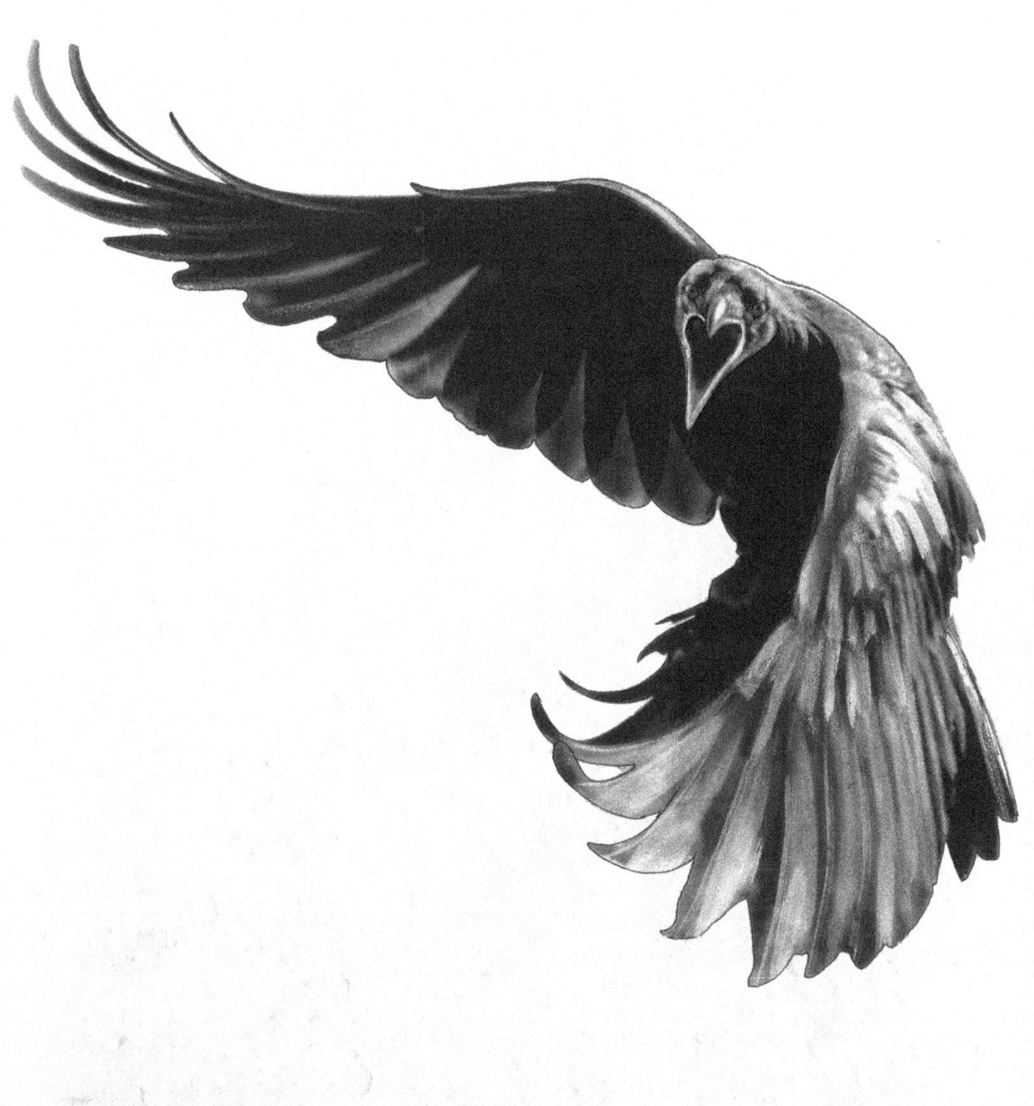

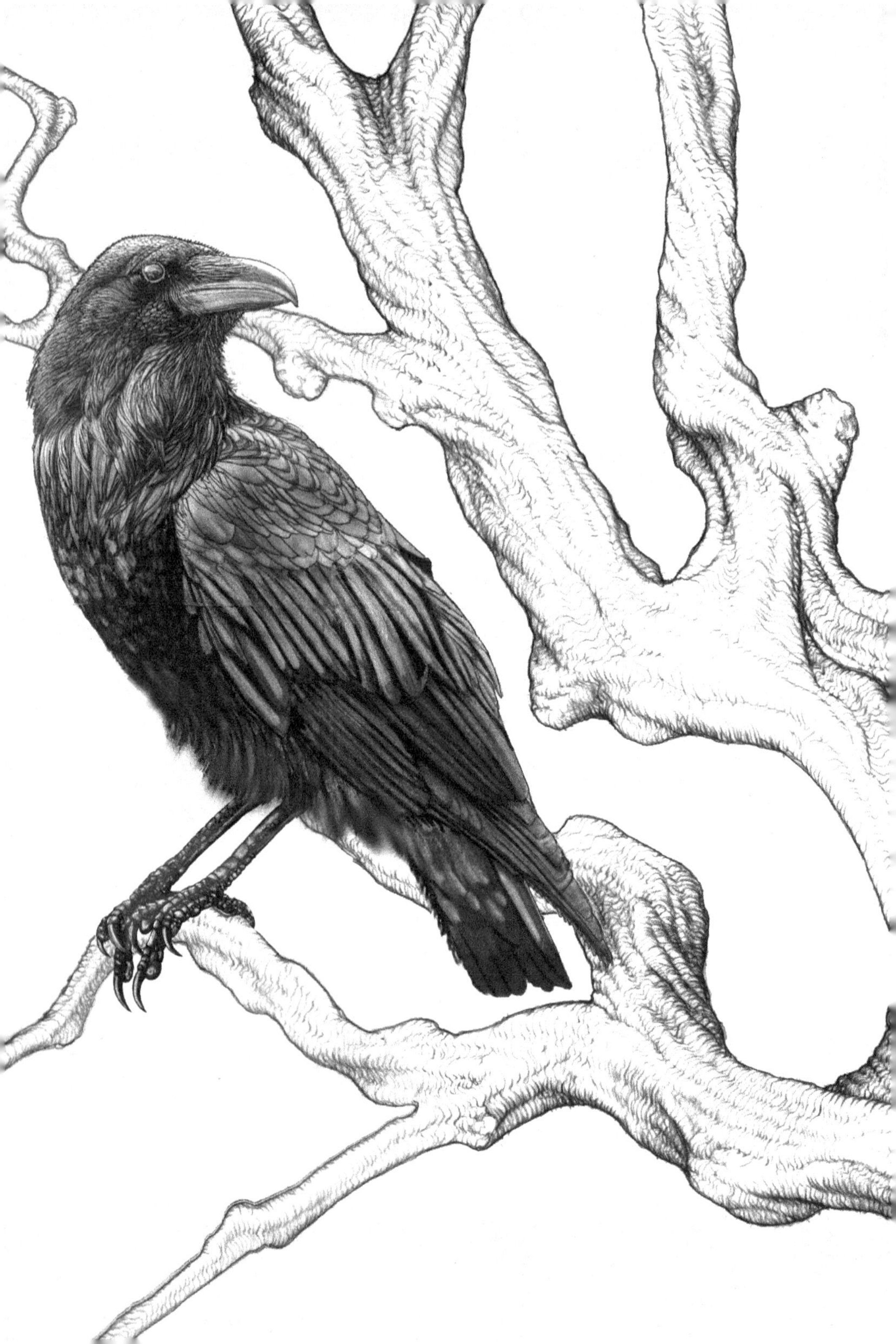

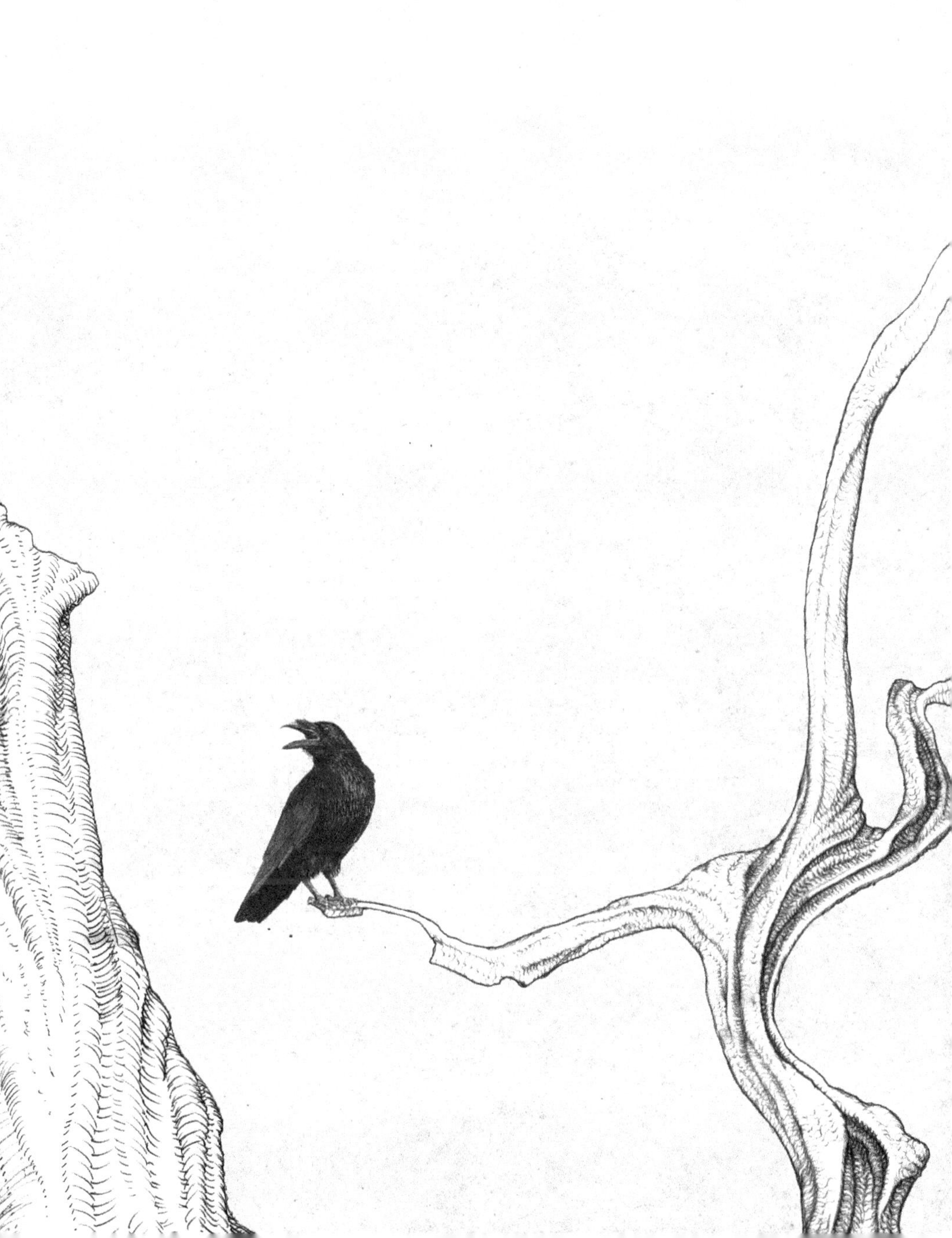

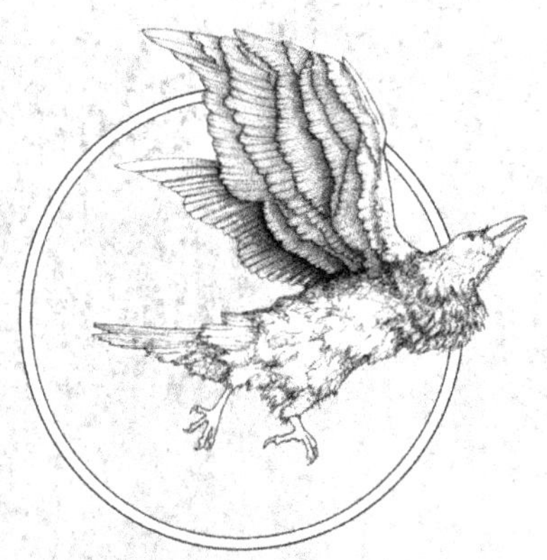

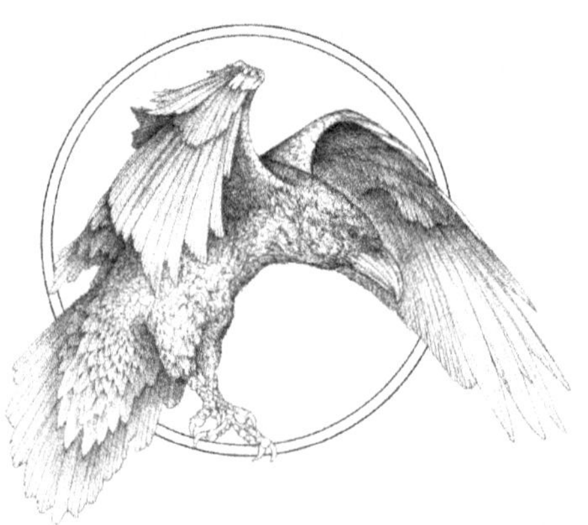

Tonight this tower
a prison seems,
though obedient to my will
and ready, at my wish,
to lie down, or move,
to this place or that.
I long to escape
into the outer sunshine
yet know
when this tower crumbles
so will I.
These windows allow no escape,
there is no door.

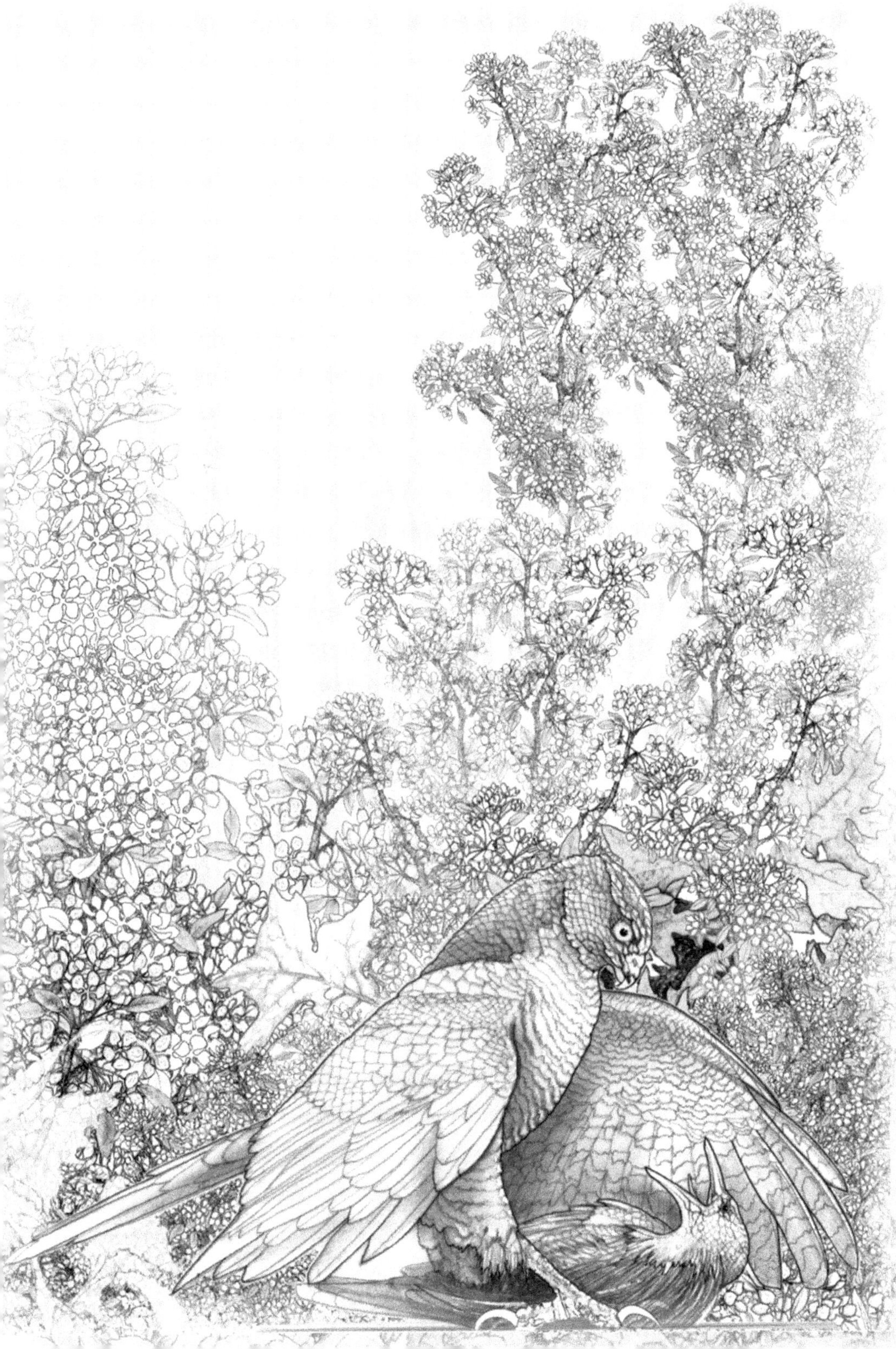

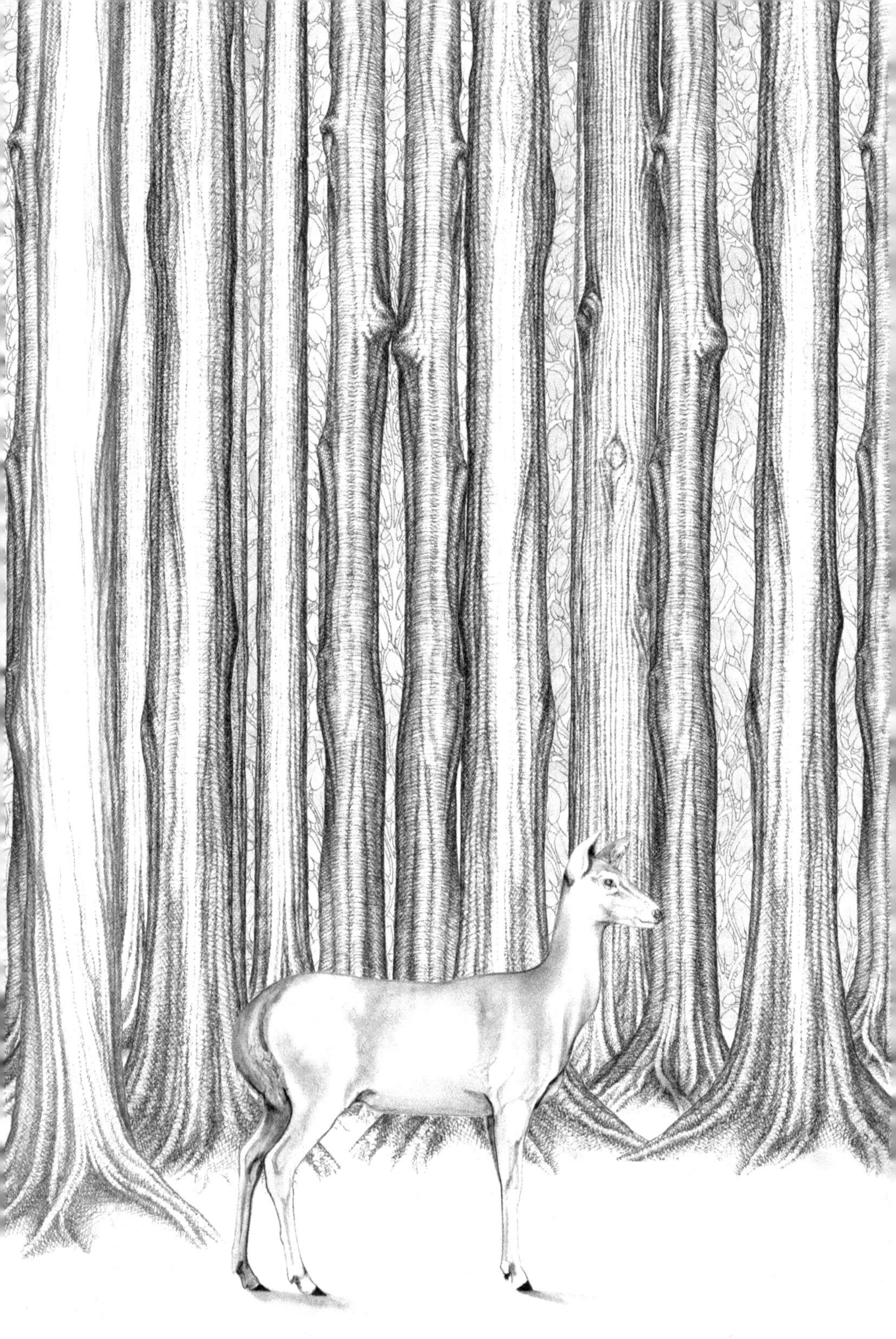

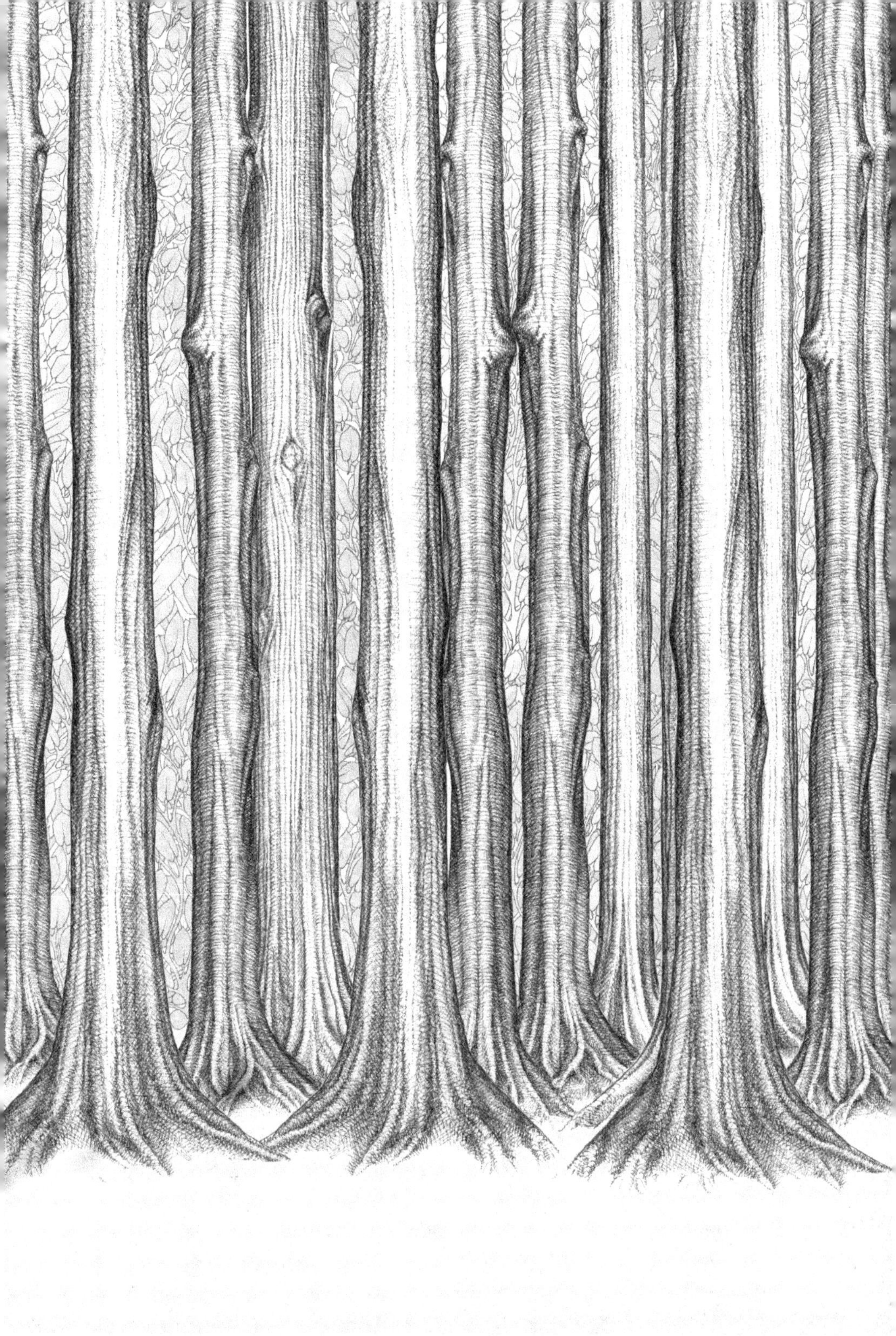

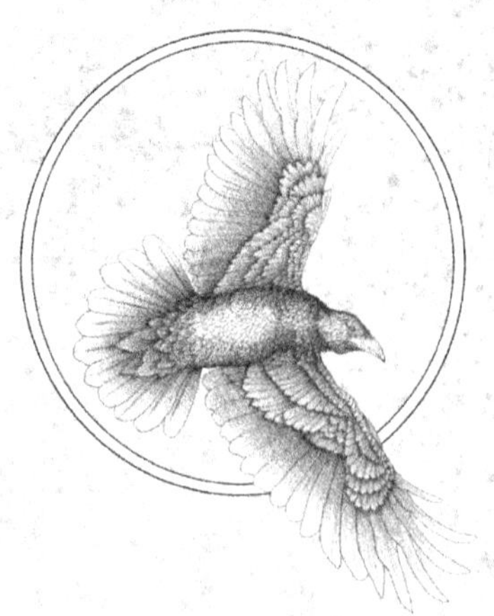

Catching at dreams,
torn from their roots,
drifting on vagrant currents
they enter a new world,
a sunlit Sargasso sea
above cold depths.

Catching at dreams,
torn from their roots,
drifting on vagrant currents
they enter a new world,
a sunlit Sargasso sea
above cold depths.

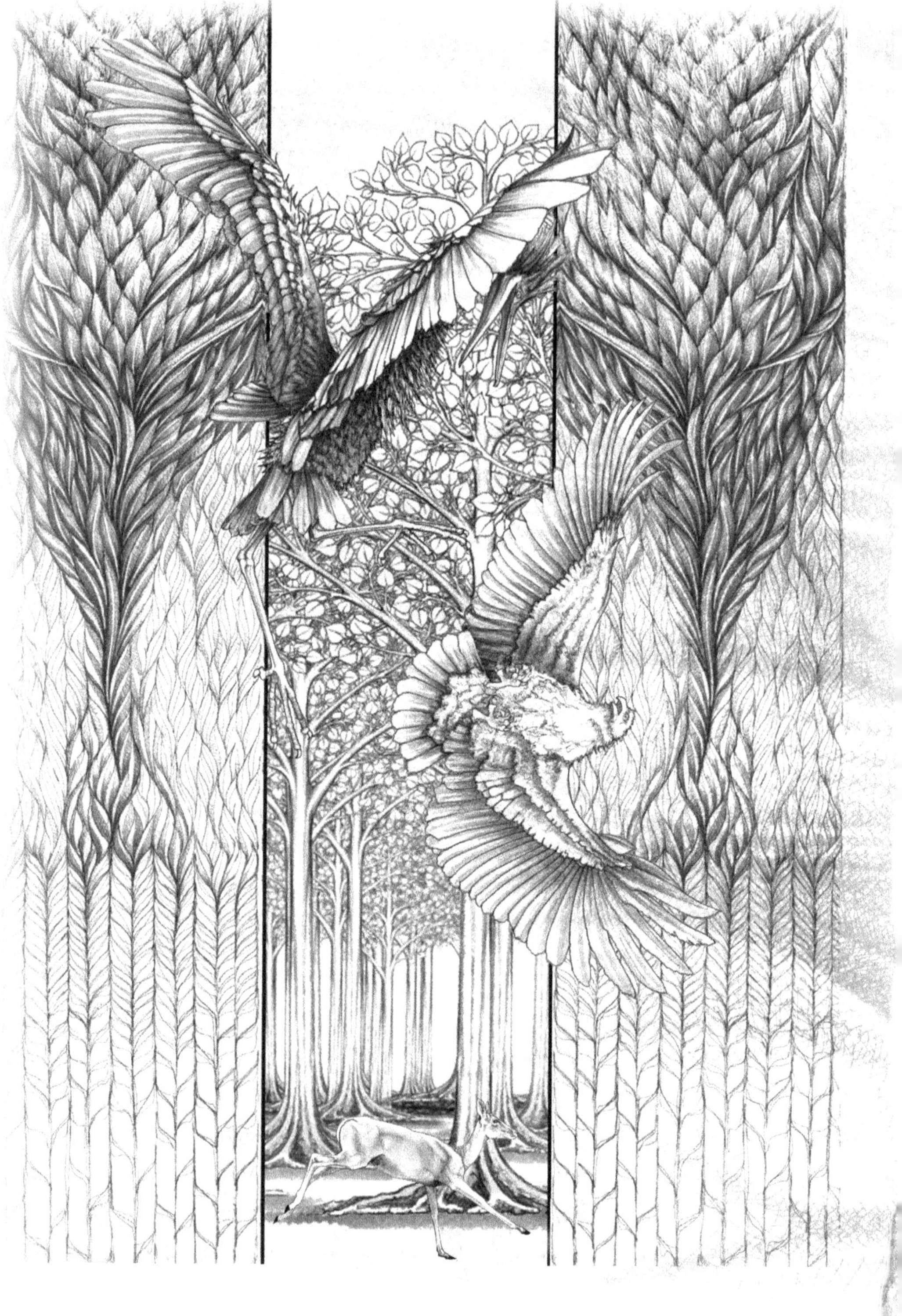

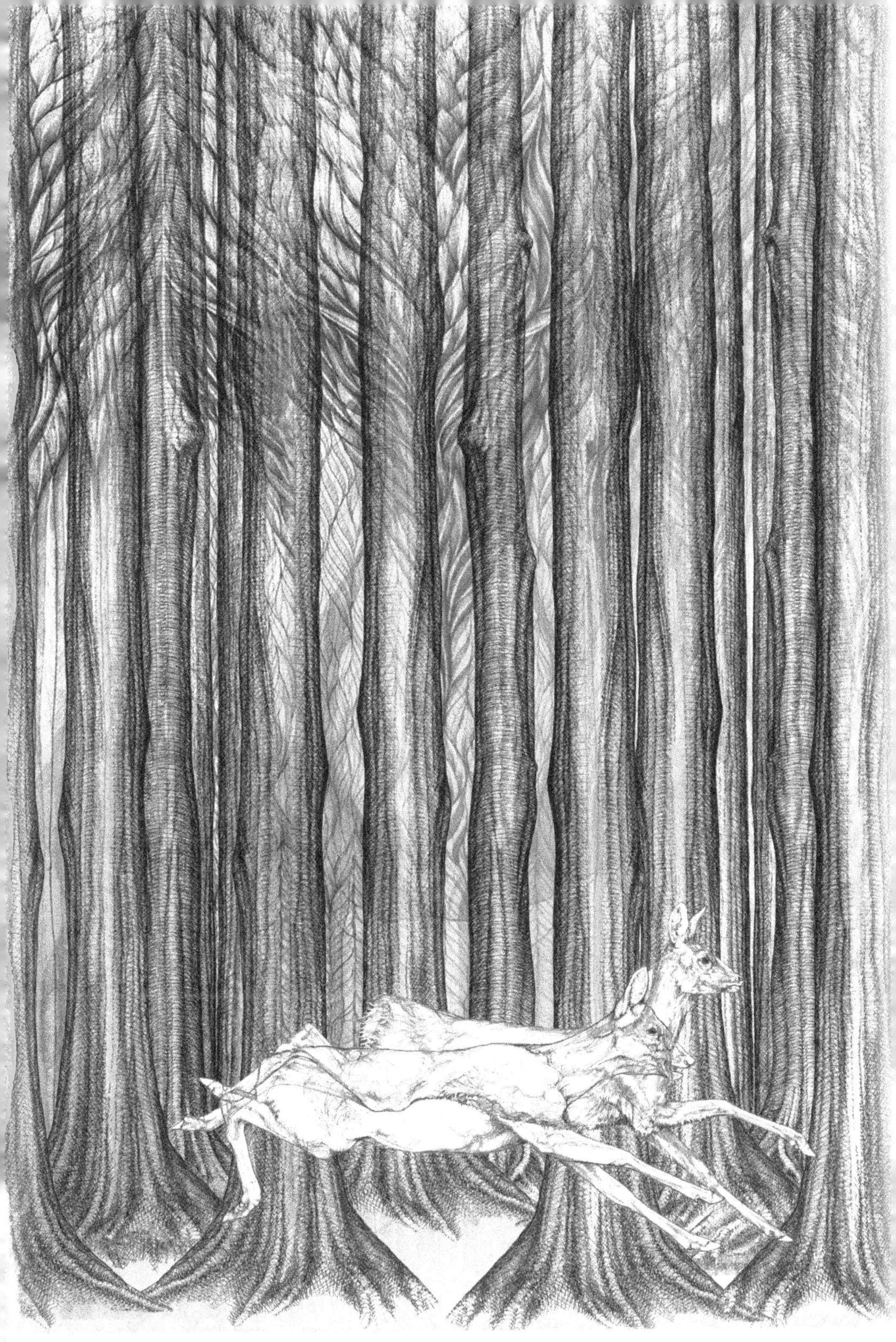

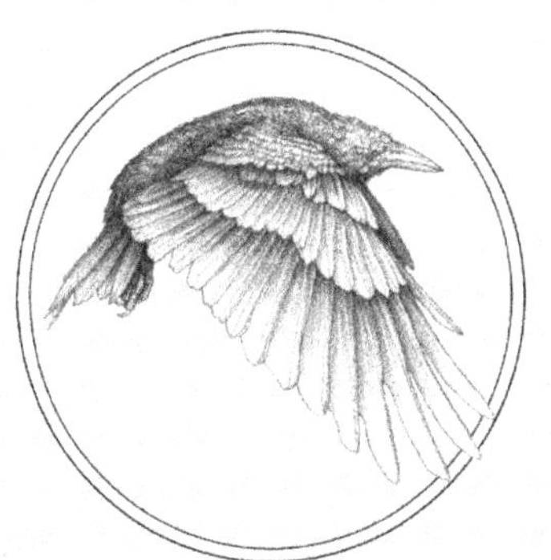

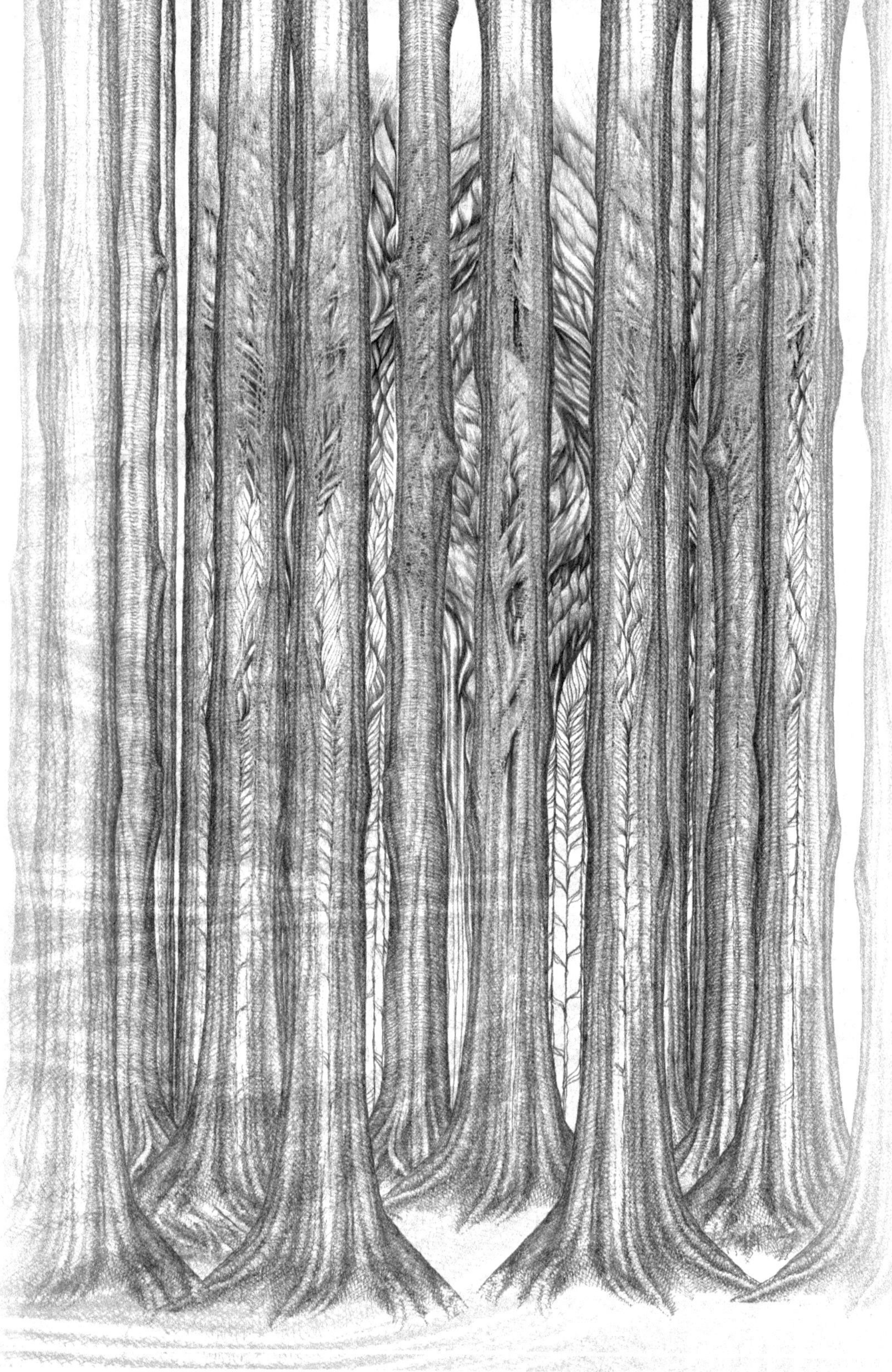

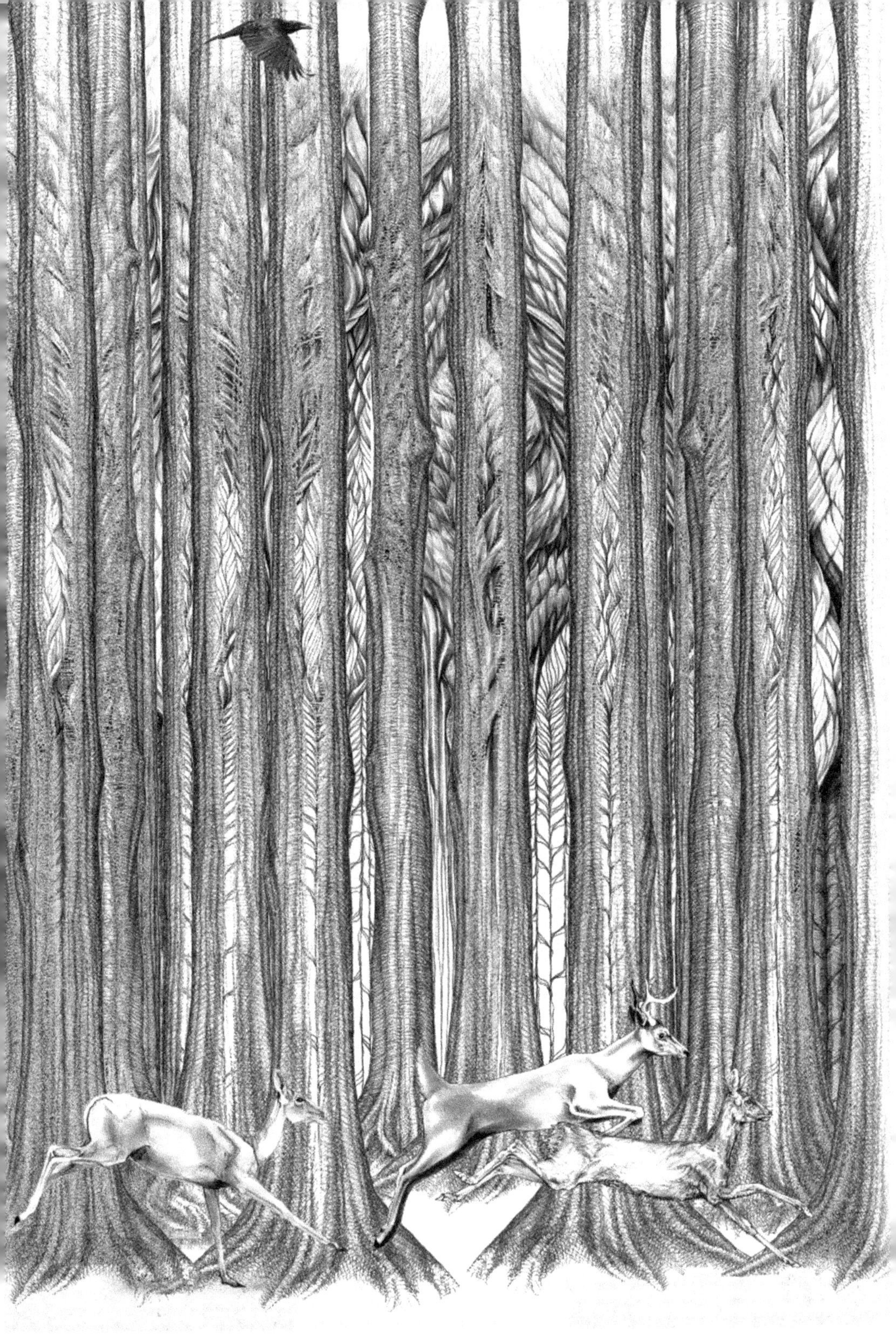

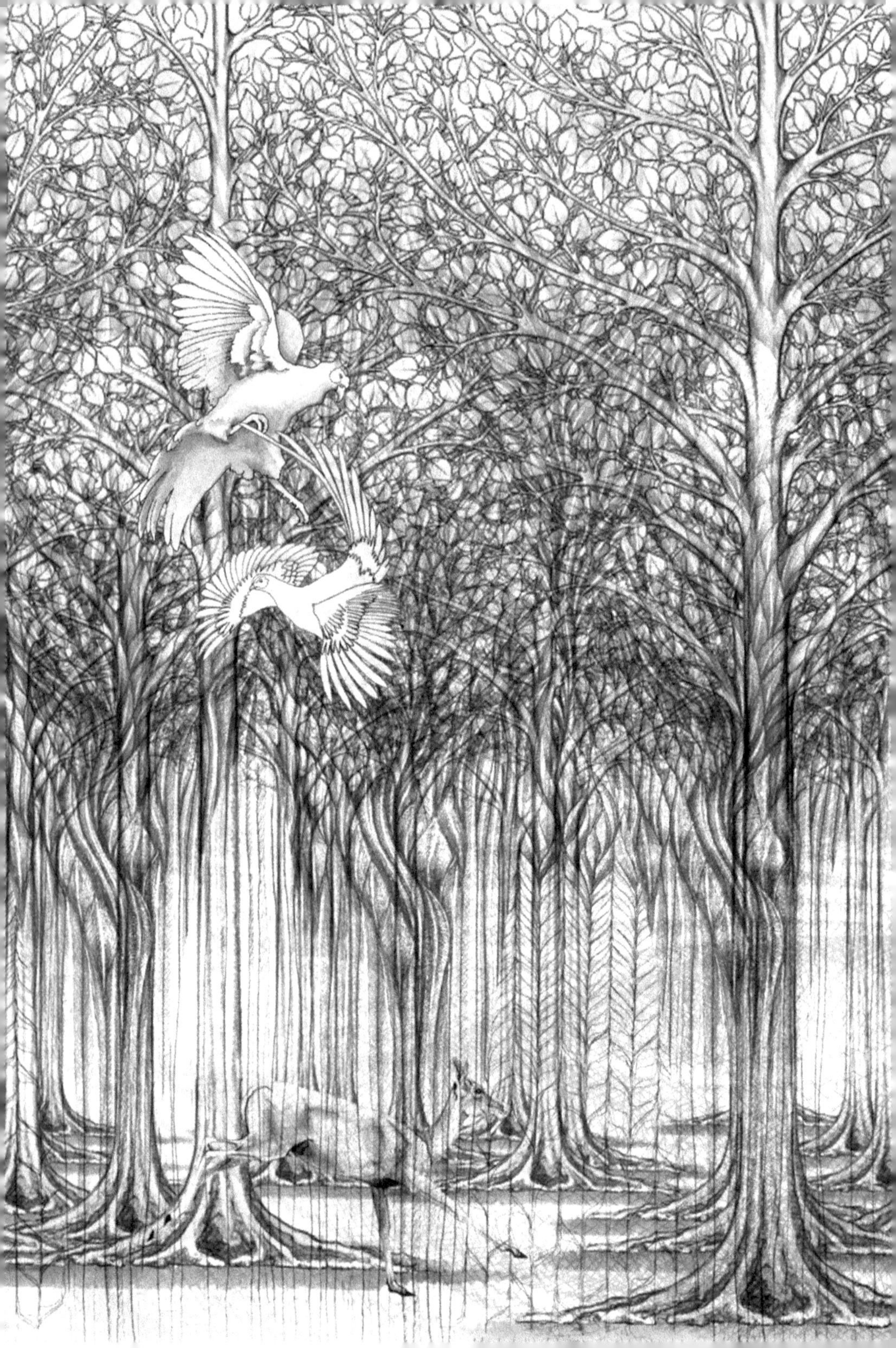

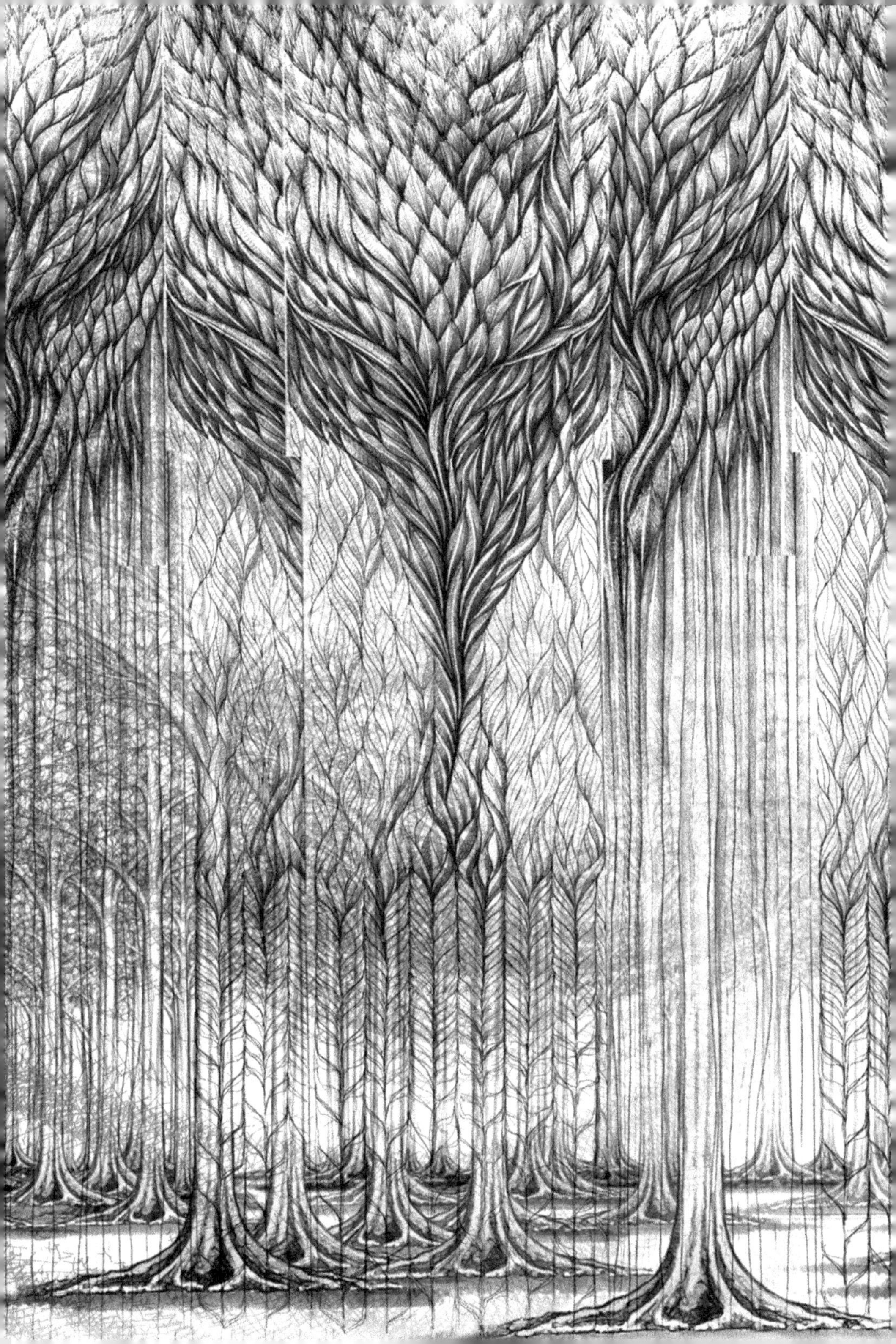

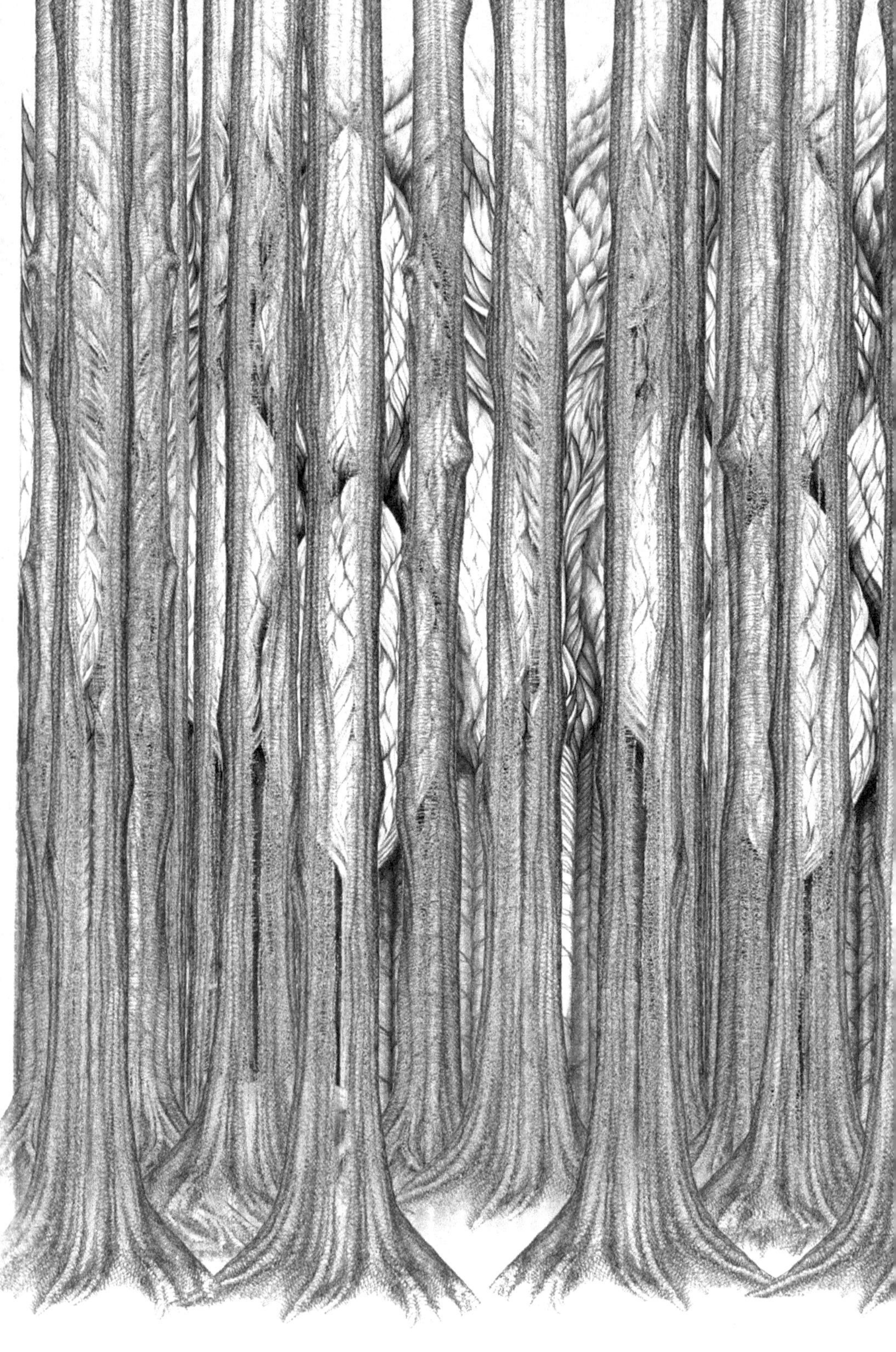

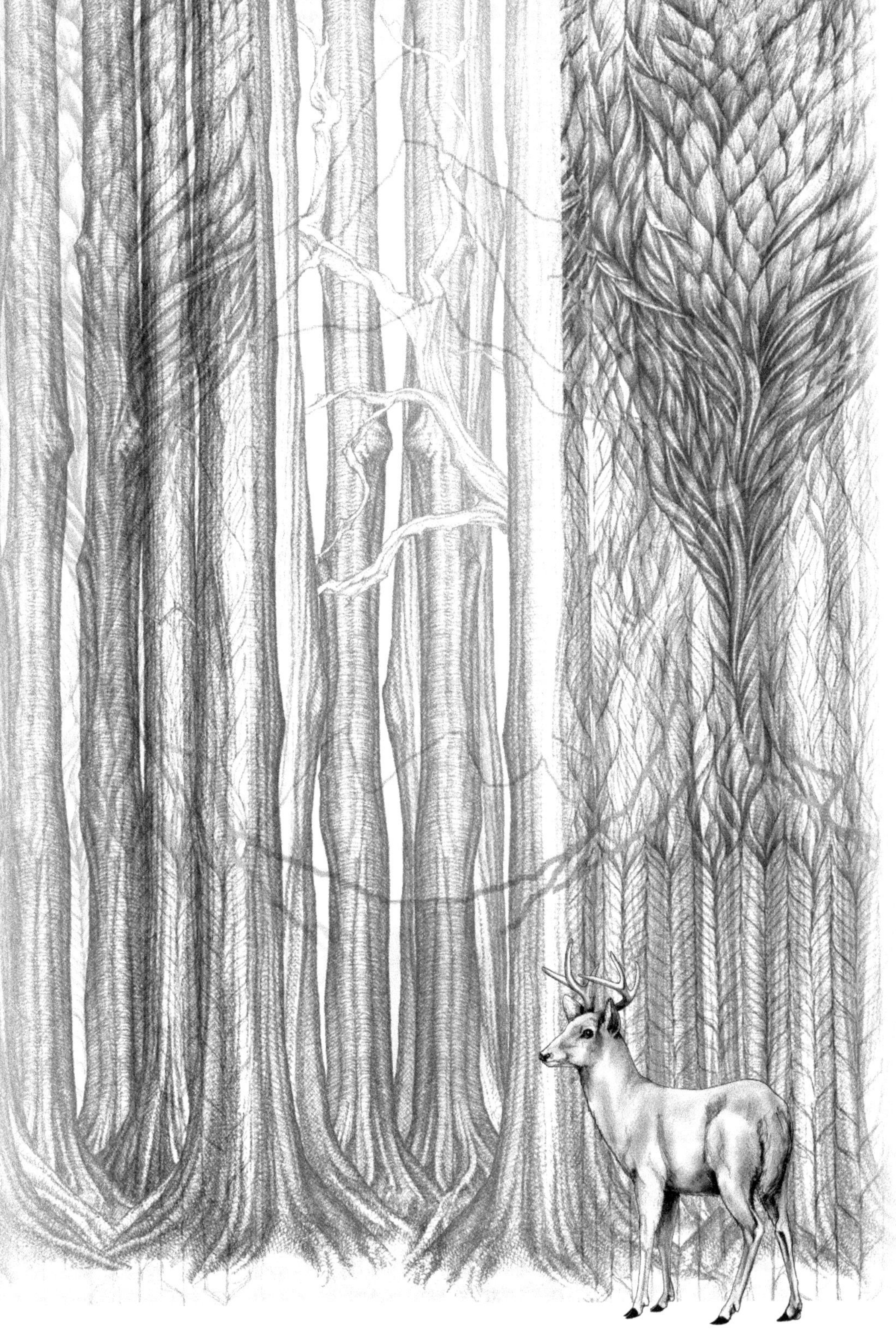

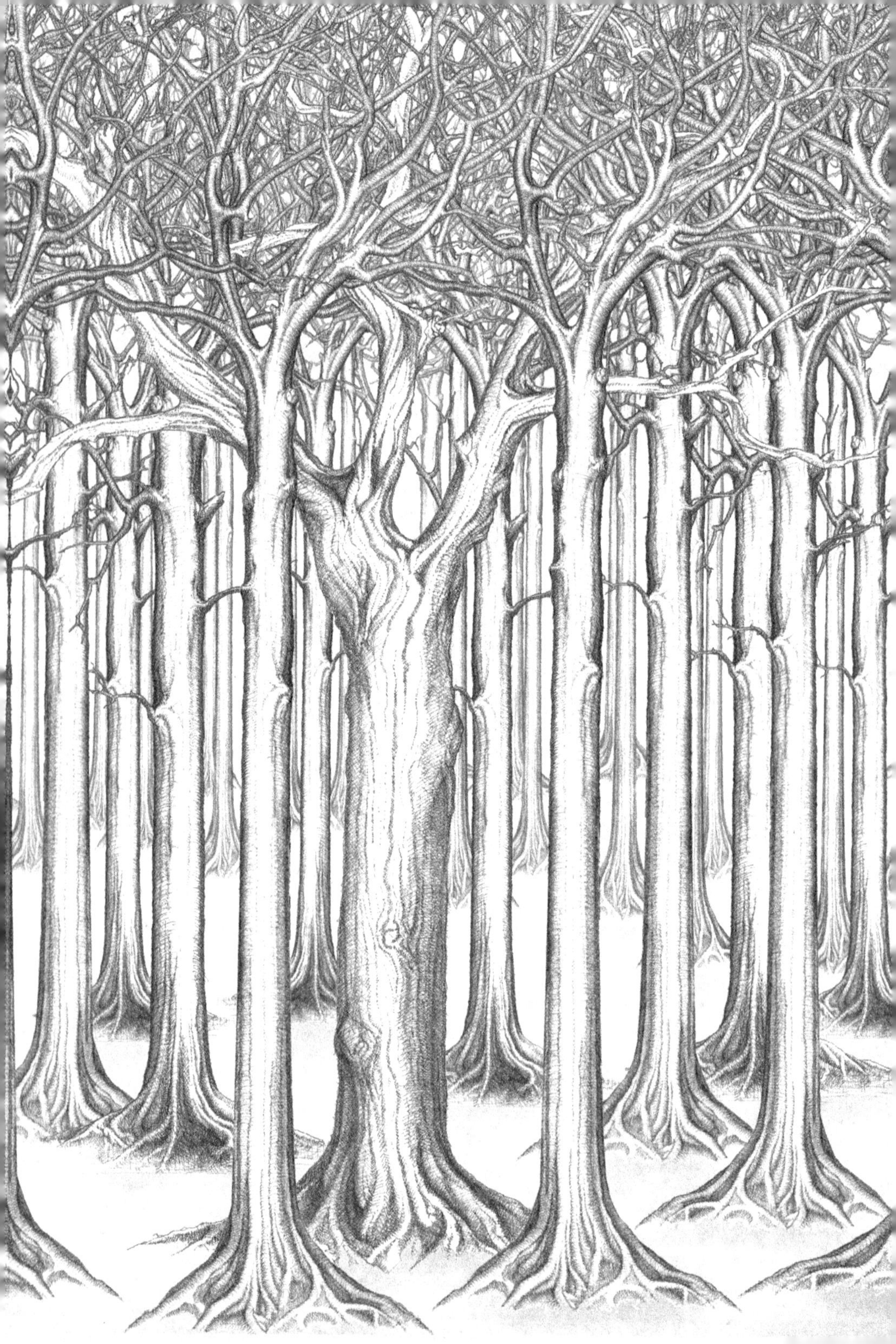

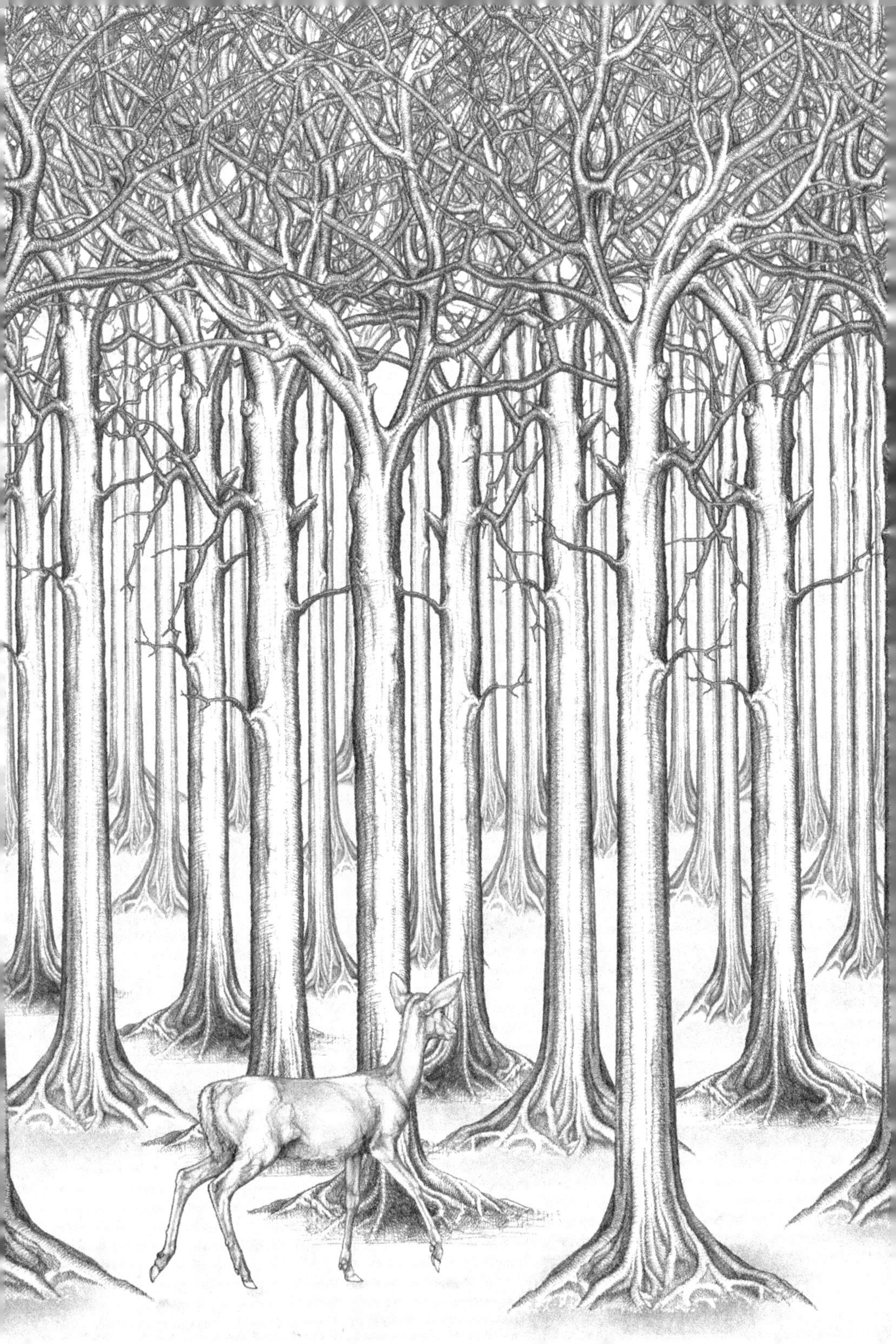

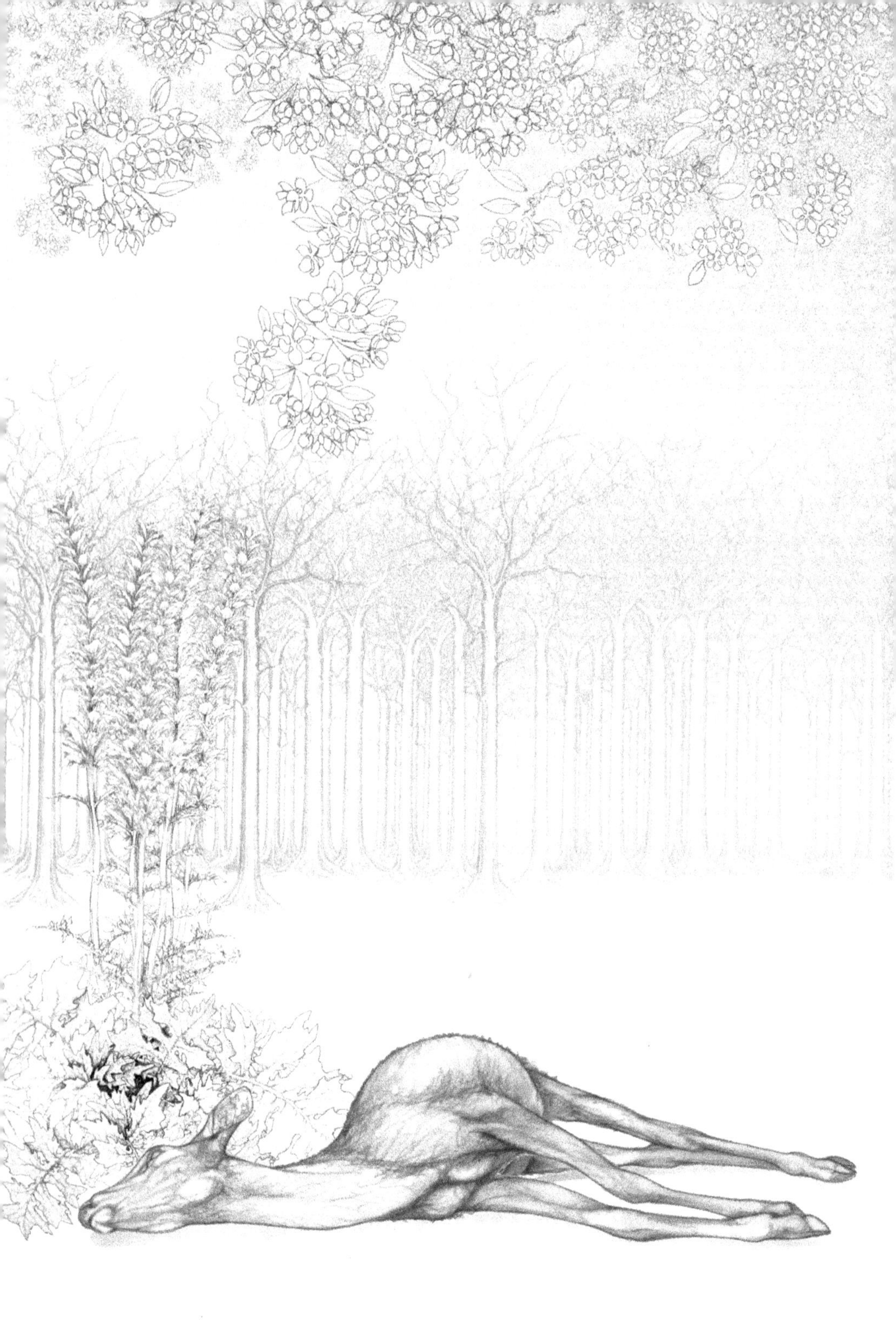

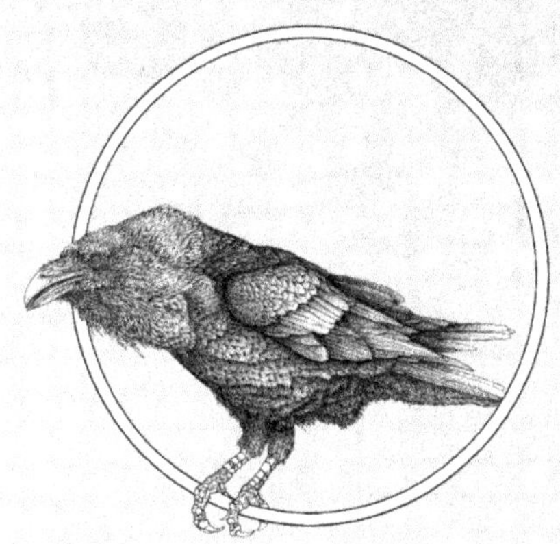

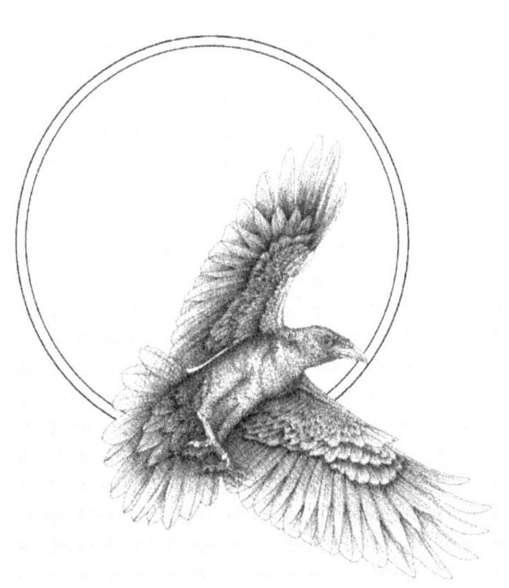

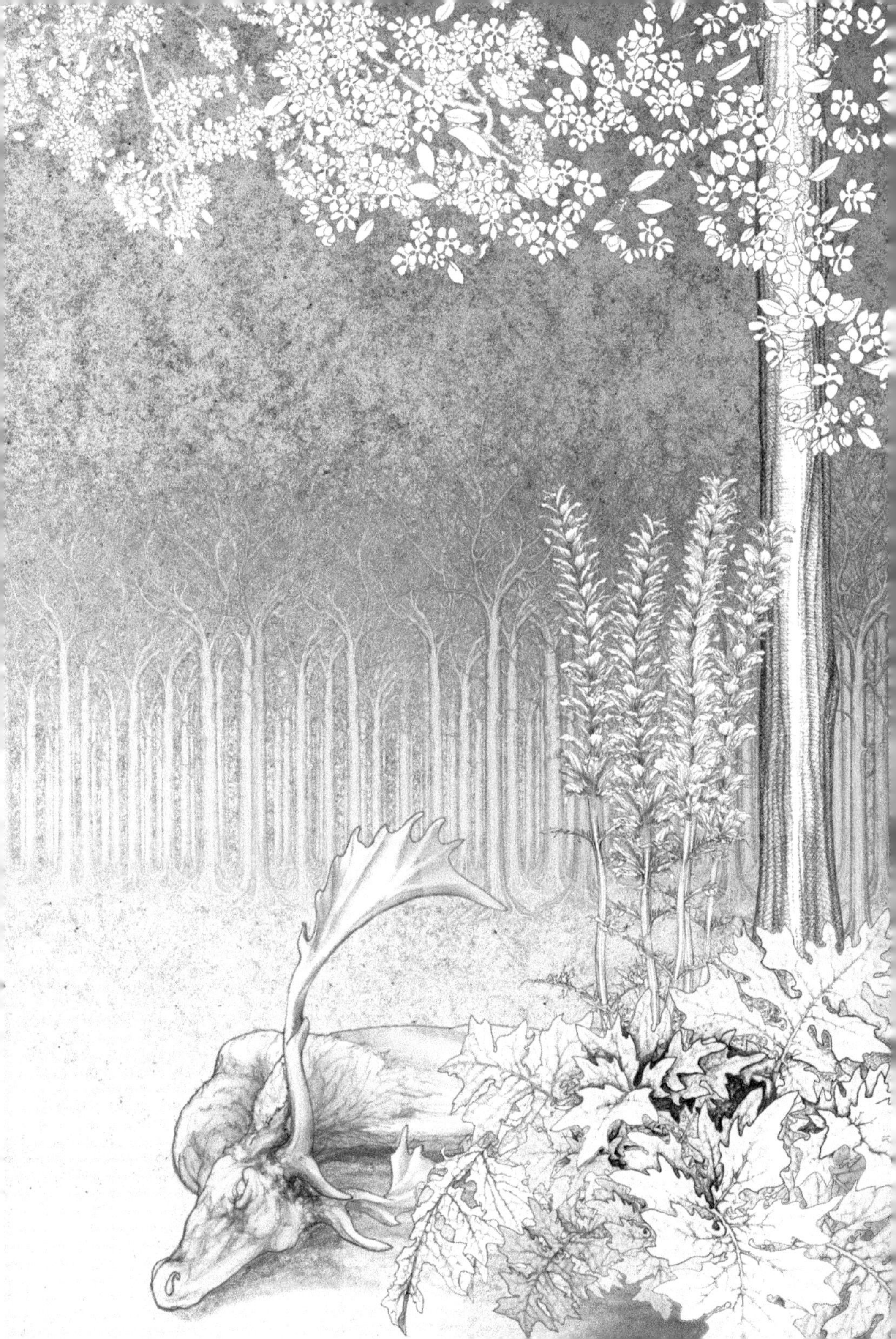

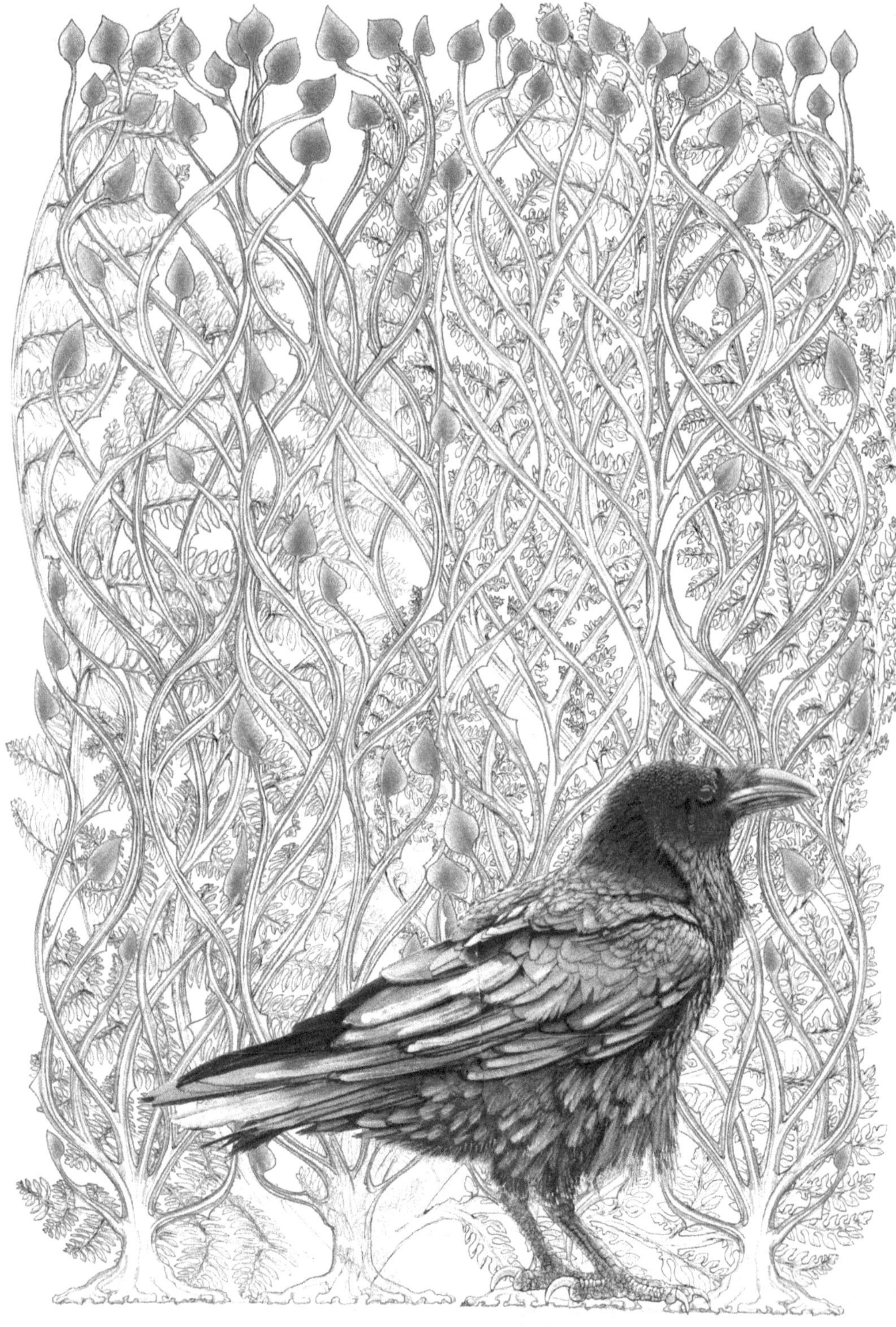

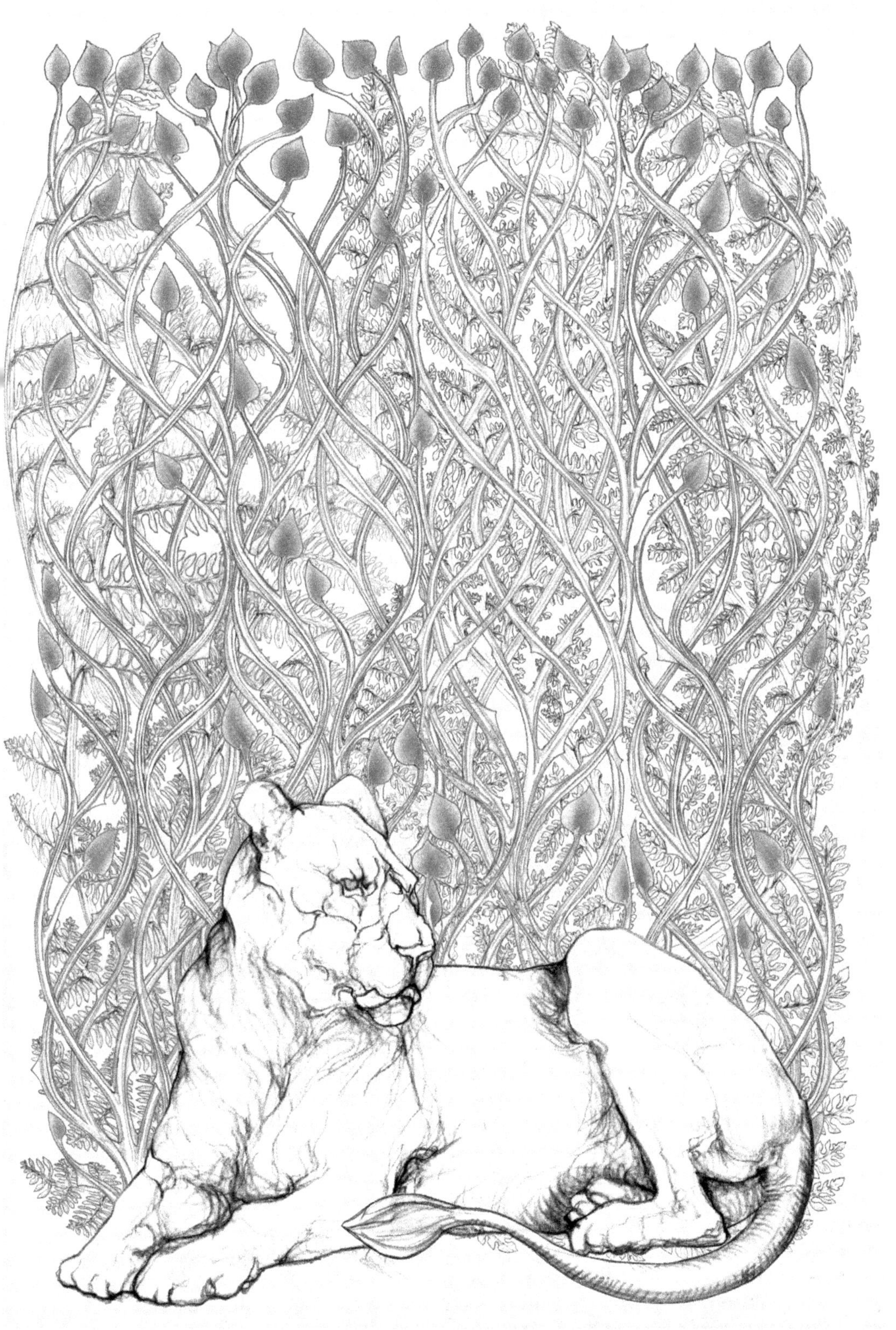

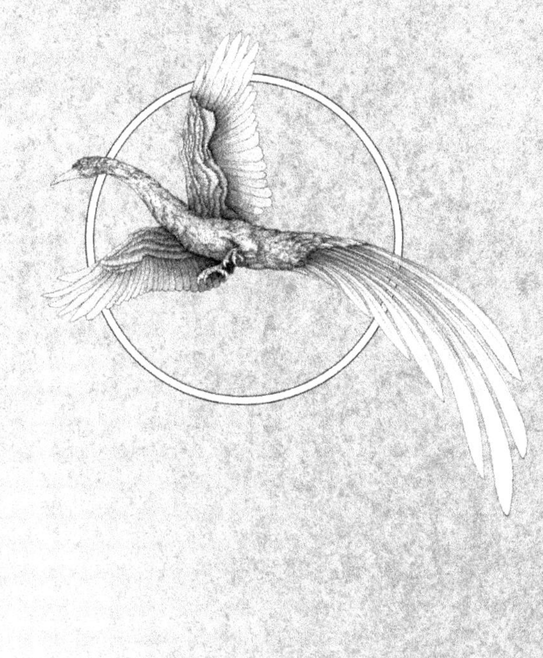

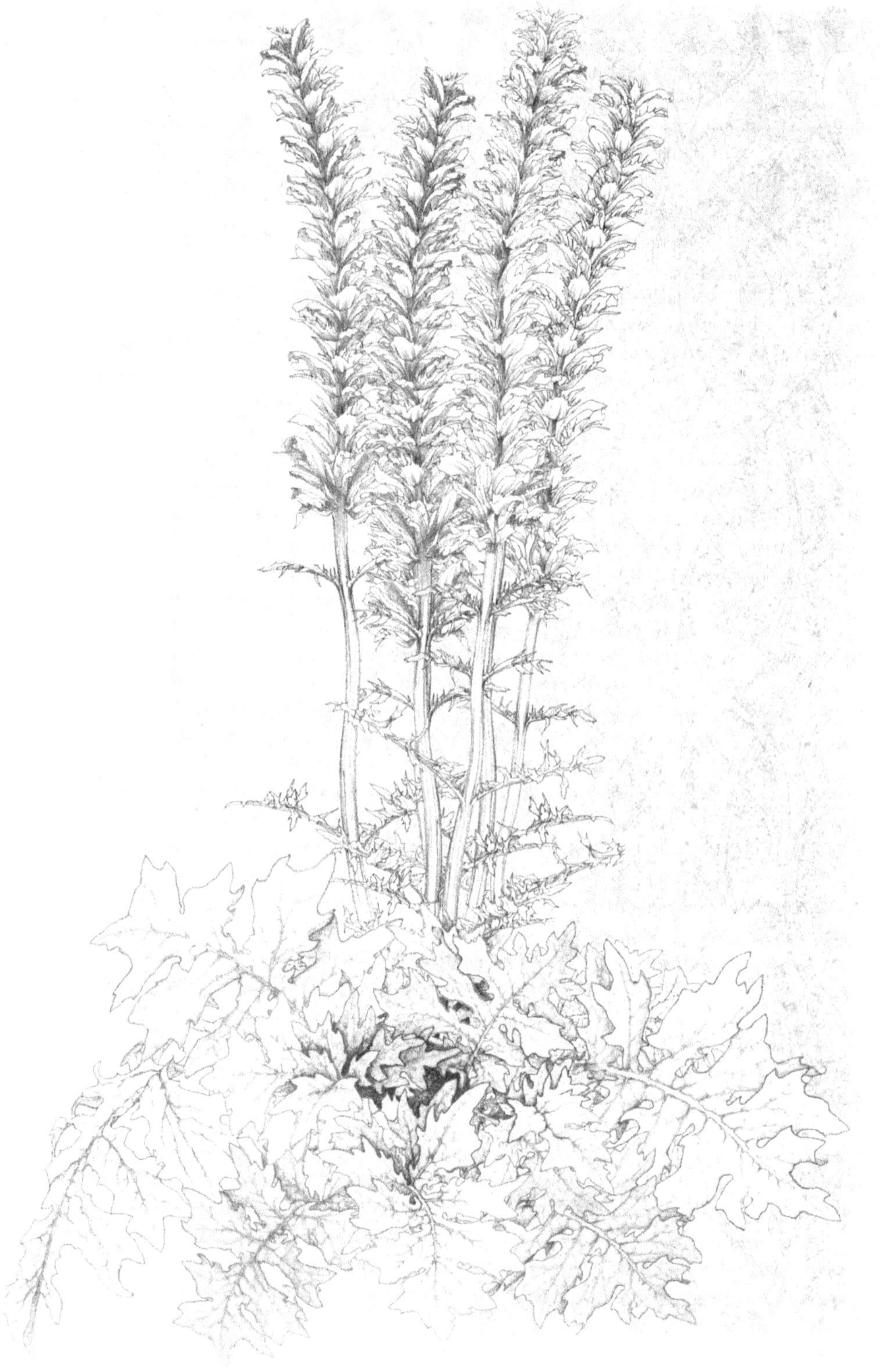

Kindness

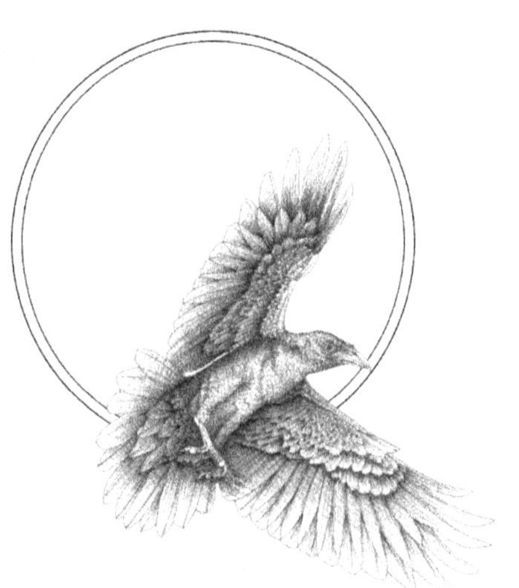

First published in Great Britain in 2023 by Wally Gilbert

Copyright © 2023 by Wally Gilbert
Illustrations by Wally Gilbert

ISBN: 978-1-912257-79-9

Instagram: Wally.Gilbert.Artist
wally_gilbert@yahoo.co.uk
www.wallygilbert.co.uk